The Revolutionary Theories of
LOUIS   AUGUSTE   BLANQUI

NUMBER 594

COLUMBIA STUDIES IN THE SOCIAL SCIENCES

EDITED BY

THE FACULTY OF POLITICAL SCIENCE

OF COLUMBIA UNIVERSITY

ALAN B. SPITZER

The Revolutionary Theories of
LOUIS AUGUSTE BLANQUI

COLUMBIA UNIVERSITY PRESS
New York   1957

Copyright © 1957 Columbia University Press, New York

Published in Great Britain, Canada, India, and Pakistan by the Oxford University Press
London, Toronto, Bombay, and Karachi

Library of Congress Catalog Card Number: 57-12573
Manufactured in the United States of America

Par./5100/3.75/7/15/68

To my father

Acknowledgments

IT GIVES ME considerable pleasure to acknowledge the help I have received in the preparation of this book. Professor Paul Beik of Swarthmore College, who first introduced me to the French revolutionary movement, has been unfailingly helpful and sympathetic. At Columbia University I have had the advantage of the rigorous supervision and warm encouragement of Professor Shepard B. Clough and the sympathetic and perceptive criticisms of Professors Jacques Barzun and Gordon Wright. The late regretted Professor Franz Neumann was an inspiring critic of the early chapters.

Monsieur Maurice Dommanget who is the unrivaled authority on Blanquism gave very graciously of his time and knowledge. Monsieur Sylvain Molinier was also extremely obliging and generous.

Without the moral and material support of my family this book could not have been written. Without the assistance, standards, and example of my wife it would have been a lesser work.

ALAN B. SPITZER

Contents

The Revolutionary Theories of
LOUIS AUGUSTE BLANQUI

The Life and Historical Role of Blanqui

THE FACT and idea of revolution have been crucial to French political history ever since 1789. Throughout the nineteenth century an articulate minority advocated the revolutionary solutions of political problems and actively fostered the resolution of ideological conflicts by physical violence. However, the great French theorists of fundamental social change, St. Simon, Fourier, Proudhon, Cabet, and their disciples, contributed a body of "socialist" ideology which repudiated the political revolutionism so eagerly espoused by the radical wing of the contemporary republican movement. The combination of revolutionism and socialist theory was a minority tendency among French radicals before 1870, and one to which few memorable figures were committed. There was, however, one socialist who not only advocated political revolution,[1] but whose career virtually embodied the revolutionary aspects of the history of nineteenth-century France. This was Louis Auguste Blanqui.

THE LIFE OF BLANQUI

Blanqui began his active political career in the conspiracy of the French Carbonari against the Restoration monarchy and concluded it as a spokesman for the socialist opposition to Gambetta's republican Opportunism. He received the

[1] See M. Ralea, *L'Idée de révolution dans les doctrines socialistes* (Paris: Jouve et Cie., 1923), p. 218: "Blanqui's primary importance rests in having transmitted the tactics of radical republicanism to socialism."

first of many wounds in 1827, during street demonstrations against Charles X,[2] and died in 1881, immediately after speaking at a mass meeting for total amnesty of the Communards.[3] He spent forty of his seventy-six years in the prisons of all the regimes which governed France from 1830 through 1881. Blanqui faced every government as an implacable critic who was always ready to translate criticism into subversive political action. His star shone most brightly during those periods of social unrest and political violence which distinguished the history of nineteenth-century France, but on the day that "order" was restored Blanqui would take his stand among the partisans of *révolution à outrance,* an object of hatred and fear to the erstwhile revolutionaries who desired merely to consolidate what they had already won. Blanqui's commitment to a permanent revolution against all feudal, religious, and capitalist institutions condemned him to a role of perpetual opposition and guaranteed his political martyrdom, or impotence, depending upon one's point of view.

Blanqui was born at Puget-Théniers in the Alpes Maritimes on February 1, 1805. He was the second son of Dominique Blanqui, a former Girondist *conventionnel* and Napoleonic functionary whose job and security disappeared with the First Empire. The small income of the young and beautiful Mme Blanqui enabled the family to send their brilliant sons Adolphe and Louis Auguste to be educated in Paris. There Blanqui received a classical education and, after leaving the *lycée* laden with honors, supported himself as a private tutor while he undertook the study of

2 H. Castille, "L. A. Blanqui," *Portraits politiques et historiques au dix-neuvième siècle* (Paris: Ferdinand Sartorius, 1857), p. 9.

3 M. Dommanget, *Blanqui* (Paris: Libraririe de l'Humanité, 1924), p. 44.

both law and medicine.[4] As a young student he developed
a passion for politics which involved him with the Carbonari. These early political years probably had a lasting
influence on his ideas of revolutionary technique. His
biographer, Geffroy, has observed:

Blanqui, introduced to politics under the Restoration, assumed
the habits of a conspirator of the Restoration period, and the
Carbonarist cell became for him the ideal type of the secret society and of possible political opposition.[5]

He was one of the leaders of Paris student agitation during the last years of the Restoration, and was wounded
three times during riots in 1827. He was in Paris, working
as a parliamentary reported for the liberal journal, the
Globe, when the Revolution of July, 1830, began. When
the Paris workers poured into the streets to destroy the
Bourbon monarchy, Blanqui scornfully left his vacillating
and legalistic employers at the office of the *Globe* and
plunged into the maelstrom, brandishing a rifle and the
tricolor.[6] For his part in the "three glorious days" of the
Revolution he was later awarded the "Decoration of July"
by Louis Philippe. This was the last award, aside from
prison sentences, that he was ever to receive from the
French government.

Almost immediately after the Revolution, Blanqui joined
the radical opposition to the July Monarchy and soon
aligned himself with a small minority of young republicans
who demanded a complete social revolution which would

4 Blanqui's older brother, the conservative economist Adolphe
Blanqui, wrote a touching account of this early period. J. A. Blanqui,
"Souvenirs d'un etudiant sous la Restauration," *Revue de Paris* (Nov.-
Dec., 1918), pp. 159-61.

5 G. Geffroy, *L'Enfermé* (Paris: Les Éditions G. Crès et Cie., 1926),
I, 38. When the entire work cited is not a translation, the translation
in the text is the author's.

6 For his own impression of these events, see pp. 132-33 below.

free the poor from economic, as well as political, thralldom. Although Blanqui was not the only republican of the period to characterize the political struggle as a struggle between social classes, he seems to have formulated most precisely the vague revolutionary demands for social, or class, justice.

In 1832, he defended himself at the trial of the republican Société des Amis du Peuple in a speech which has been described as "the first socialist manifesto of this epoch." [7] When Blanqui was asked at this trial to give his profession, he made the famous reply: "Proletarian . . . the class of thirty million Frenchmen who live by their labor and who are deprived of political rights." [8]   The eloquent young firebrand was acquitted by the jury, but sentenced to one year in prison for his attempt, in the words of the court, "to trouble the public peace by arousing the contempt and hatred of the citizenry against several classes of people which he had variously described as the privileged rich or the *bourgeoisie*." [9]

Upon his release from prison Blanqui plunged into the old Carbonarist atmosphere of clandestine organization which was revived as the Orleanist government severely curtailed freedom of association. He founded a secret revolutionary "Society of Families" in 1834, but his careful organization was shattered when he and the other leaders of the society were arrested in 1836 for the illegal possession of arms.[10]

[7] J. Tchernoff, *Le Parti républicain sous la Monarchie de Juillet* (Paris: A. Pedone, 1901), p. 261.

[8] Société des Amis du Peuple, *Procès des Quinze* (Paris: Imprimerie de Auguste Mie, 1832), p. 3.

[9] *Ibid.*, p. 148.

[10] This organization was described in detail by the public prosecutor Mérilhou at Blanqui's trial in 1839, Cours des Pairs, *Affaire des 12 and 13 Mai, 1839* (Paris: Imprimerie Royale, 1839), pp. 9-30.

When the amnesty of 1837 released him from prison Blanqui returned to Paris, for him the only possible arena of the class struggle. There, with the aid of two popular young republicans, Armand Barbès and Martin Bernard, he established another organization, "The Society of Seasons." Classic conspiratorial techniques were utilized to form a tightly disciplined and hierarchical organization. The small isolated cells of the rank and file received orders from subaltern leaders who themselves were unaware of the identity of the mysterious directors of the conspiracy. All of the conspirators were sworn to unquestioning obedience. From time to time the small individual groups assembled in the streets at the word of their immediate superiors without ever knowing which call was to be the signal for the real coup.

During the economic and political crisis of May, 1839, Blanqui decided to make his attempt. On the twelfth of May, the little band of students and workers formed in the streets, broke into arsenals and gunshops, and tried to carry the city's key positions. The Paris of workers and artisans which was expected to transform the insurrection into a revolution stood by silently and apathetically while government troops easily crushed the rising.[11] Blanqui evaded arrest for a few months but was finally captured, tried by the Chamber of Peers, and sentenced to death.[12] His sentence was commuted to deportation by Louis Philippe, and he was sent to join most of his comrades in the prison-fortress of Mont-Saint-Michel.

For nine years he lived the role for which he is probably

[11] A book has been devoted to this effort: A. Zévaès, *Une Révolution manquée* (Paris: Éditions de la Nouvelle Revue Critique, 1933). See also M. Dommanget, "Auguste Blanqui et l'insurrection du 12 Mai 1839," *La Critique Sociale*, XI (March, 1934), 233-45.

[12] *La Gazette des Tribunaux*, July 13-14, 1840.

best remembered—*L'Enfermé*, the imprisoned one, the suffering but uncompromising hostage of the conservative forces of five successive regimes. The little society of the political prisoner, with its hopeless defiance of a barbarous prison administration, its perpetual effort to preserve a shred of personal integrity under the most degrading conditions, and its bitter and self-consuming factional struggles, was isolated and politically ineffectual, but an object of widespread interest and sympathy.

Blanqui remained a prisoner, at Mont-Saint-Michel,[13] and then at Tours, until 1848, when the February Revolution released him and brought him hurrying to the center of the Paris stage. By this time the myth of Blanqui as the sinister incarnation of bloodthirsty anarchism was held not only by the good conservative families of France, but by most of his more moderate colleagues in the republican movement as well. Tocqueville's description of Blanqui at the rostrum of the National Assembly on May 15, 1848, is a fair picture of how this revolutionary appeared to the conservative politicians:

It was then that I saw appear in his turn on the tribune a man whom I have never seen since, but the recollection of whom has always filled me with horror and disgust. He had wan, emaciated cheeks, white lips, a sickly wicked and repulsive expression, a dirty pallor, the appearance of a moldy corpse; he wore no visible linen; an old black frock coat tightly covered his lean withered limbs; he seemed to have passed his life in a sewer and to have just left it. I was told it was Blanqui.[14]

13 F. Girard, *Histoire du Mont Saint-Michel* (Paris: Paul Permain et Cie., 1849); L. Noguès, *Une Condamnation de Mai 1839* (Paris: J. Bry Ainé, 1850).

14 A. de Tocqueville, *Recollections*, tr. A. T. de Mattos (New York: Columbia University Press, 1949), p. 130. Cf. V. Hugo, *Souvenirs personnels, 1848-1851*, ed. H. Guillemin (Paris: Gallimard, 1952), pp. 167-70.

A considerably different idea of Blanqui was cherished by a small but devoted coterie of disciples. To them this small, ascetic, prematurely aged man had unstintingly given his health and freedom to an ideal, and received and expected no rewards but prison, hatred, and contumely. Many more objective observers were impressed by his apparently exclusive and selfless devotion to a cause and by the magnetism of his dedicated personality. Delvau, who had been Ledru-Rollin's secretary, in his *Histoire de la Révolution de Février* described his personal impressions of Blanqui in 1848 as follows:

At first sight Blanqui does not appear very attractive, but that is because suffering is not always very agreeable to watch. One is disposed to obey him, but not to love him. He does not attract, he dominates. Blanqui replaces the physical strength that he lacks with a virility of the soul, which on certain occasions is all-powerful.[15]

As soon as he had arrived in Paris, Blanqui formed a club to organize the dissatisfaction of the extreme radicals with what they considered the potentially counterrevolutionary activity of the Provisional Government. Apparently Blanqui eschewed revolutionary conspiracy while attempting to force the government to the left by the pressure of speeches, journals, and mass demonstrations.[16] The provisional government, including its most radical members, repaid Blanqui's mistrust with fear and hatred. His growing influence was undermined by the publication of a document alleged to have been copied from a confession made by Blanqui which gave Louis Philippe's police in-

15 A. Delvau, *Histoire de la Révolution de Février* (Paris: Garnier Frères, 1850), I, 318.
16 A very fine work on Blanqui's role in 1848 is: S. Wasserman, *Les Clubs de Barbès et de Blanqui* (Paris: Édouard Cornély et Cie., 1913).

formation about the conspiracy of 1839.[17] The accusation
has never been decisively proved or disproved, but the sup-
porting testimony of Barbès, Blanqui's former fellow conspirator who had become his bitterest enemy, struck a
sharp blow to his prestige among the Paris militants.[18]

The tensions among the disparate groups which had
taken over the heritage of the July Monarchy were height-
ened as the attempts of the Provisional Government to establish order according to moderate middle-class principles
were met by the street demonstrations and incendiary
manifestoes of the Paris radicals. The continuous agitation bore fruit on May 15, when a mob invaded the pre-
cincts of the newly elected and quite conservative Constitu-
ent Assembly. What had begun as a demonstration for a
revolutionary war against the Russian oppression of Poland
became an attempt to overthrow the government. Blanqui
was reluctantly involved in the inception of this movement, but did not join the mob when it made its way to
the Hôtel de Ville to proclaim a revolutionary government.[19] Nevertheless, he was imprisoned along with most
of the socialists and radical leaders after this improvised
insurrection had been crushed by the bourgeois National
Guard. Therefore he was unable to join the Paris workers
in their last desperate attempt to achieve a social revolution in the bloody "June days" of 1848.

17 This document was published by a certain Taschereau in *Revue
Retrospective* (Paris: Paulin, 1848), pp. 3-10. It is often referred to
as the "Taschereau Document."

18 A strong partisan of Blanqui has written a rather persuasive book
mustering the evidence, although not the absolute proof, of Blanqui's
complete innocence of the charge: M. Dommanget, *Une Drame politique en 1848* (Paris: Les Deux Sirènes, 1948). For the opposite point
of view: J. F. Jeanjean, *Armand Barbès* (Paris: Édouard Cornély et
Cie., 1909), I, 159-70.

19 For a more detailed account of these events, see pp. 150-52 below.

Throughout the next decade Blanqui languished in various republican and imperial prisons. There he read, lectured on political economy, and led his disciples in demonstrations against the prison authorities. A great deal of his energy was spent in factional clashes with fellow prisoners—disputes common to socialist politics. He was not entirely forgotten by the outside world for he managed to shock liberal opinion by condemnations of all of those republicans and moderate socialists, including Louis Blanc, who had in his opinion betrayed the workers in 1848. He emerged at this time as perhaps the first socialist "anti-participationist" who demands the absolute proletarian purity of his party.[20]

In 1859 Blanqui was released from prison and went straight to Paris to do battle with the Second Empire. By 1861 he was back in jail, sentenced to four years for "conspiracy." [21] During this period he met and influenced a new generation of young intellectuals who had been imprisoned for various crimes against the security of the state. Some of them, "Blanquists of the second rank," admired him without accepting his complete domination. In this group were Clemenceau and Ranc, among others, who were to become the stalwarts of the Radical Socialist Party.[22] Other young militants subordinated themselves completely to the will of *le Vieux* and were the nucleus for a devoted revolutionary general staff after Blanqui escaped from a prison hospital in 1865.[23]

[20] There is a very full account of this period, including several important documents, in M. Dommanget, *Auguste Blanqui à Belle-Ile* (Paris: Librairie du Travail, 1935).

[21] *La Gazette des Tribunaux,* June 14, 1861.

[22] A. Ranc, *Souvenirs—Correspondance 1831-1908* (Paris: Édouard Cornély et Cie., 1913), p. 27.

[23] See Paul Lafargue's appreciation, "Auguste Blanqui—souvenirs

In these last years of the tottering Empire, Blanqui naturally did all that he could to hasten its collapse. From his refuge in Belgium he guided an expanding group of young Blanquists in the formation of a revolutionary organization along the old conspiratorial lines, equally divided among students and workers.[24] Many of Blanqui's lieutenants were to play important roles in the Commune of 1871. Eudes, Tridon, Ferré, Rigault, and other communard leaders began their revolutionary careers under the tutelage of *le Vieux,* the old master revolutionary. Blanqui slipped into Paris from time to time to direct the activities of his approximately two thousand adherents. In August, 1870, he was reluctantly compelled by the impatience of his enthusiastic disciples, and by the fear that his organization would melt away, to lead a premature assault on the tottering Second Empire.[25] Adventures of this nature have stamped him with the somewhat invidious label of "insurrectionist."

When the Empire did fall on September 4, 1870, power was immediately seized by the liberal politicians who were willing to accept a republic and eager to forestall a social revolution. They guided the country through its last hopeless writhings beneath the Prussian heel and handed it over to a National Assembly which was to arrange the surrender in approved constitutional fashion.

---

personnel," in *La Révolution Française,* April 20, 1879. Lafargue wrote: "To Blanqui belongs the honor of having made the revolutionary education of a section of the youth of our generation."

[24] C. Da Costa, *Les Blanquistes,* Vol. VI of *Histoires des partis socialistes en France* (Paris: Marcel Rivière, 1912), *passim.* Cf. M. Dommanget, "Les groupes Blanquistes de la fin du Second-Empire," *Revue Socialiste,* XLIV (Feb., 1951), 225-31.

[25] Blanqui's own description of this event appeared in his journal *La Patrie en danger.* L. A. Blanqui, *La Patrie en danger* (Paris: A. Chevalier, 1871), pp. 49-61. Cf. A. Zévaès, *Auguste Blanqui* (Paris: Marcel Rivière, 1920), pp. 216-20.

At first the Parisian radicals, including the Blanquists, had agreed to cooperate with the bourgeois government of National Defense in the face of the German menace. Blanqui, soon suspecting that the government preferred Prussian troops in Paris to armed French workers, began to attack the new administration on patriotic grounds in his newspaper *La Patrie en danger*. He had been raised in the peculiarly French atmosphere of leftist chauvinism which yearned for a war in the great revolutionary tradition, and whose main objection to conservative governments had been their relatively peaceful and internationalist outlook. When the news of the surrender of Metz impelled an angry crowd to seize the Hôtel de Ville on October 31, 1870, Blanqui followed it, and participated in the abortive attempt to set up a new government of revolutionary patriots. With this failure disappeared his last faint hope of inspiring Paris to fight a revolutionary war.[26]

Heartbroken and disgusted by the surrender to the Prussians, Blanqui left Paris in February, 1871, and retired to the country. There he was arrested for his part in the attempted coup of October, and hustled into secret confinement on March 17, the day before civil war broke out in Paris. The government of Versailles refused the offer of the Communards to exchange all of their hostages for Blanqui, who in the words of his archenemy, Thiers, "was worth an army corps." [27] The "mathematician of revolution" languished in a hidden prison while his followers fought their hopeless battle on the walls and in the streets of Paris.

[26] M. Dommanget, *Blanqui, la Guerre de 1870-71 et la Commune* (Paris: Éditions Domat, 1947), pp. 70-84.

[27] B. Flotte, *Blanqui et les otages en 1871* (Paris: Imprimerie Jeannette, 1885), p. 27.

For a few tragic months in 1871 the accumulated political
bitterness of a century was distilled into the bloody struggle
between the Paris of workers and radical intellectuals and
the France of the middle class and the Catholic peasantry.
The real nature of the Commune has been the subject of
endless controversy. Its leaders were predominantly agita-
tors and journalists of middle-class origin, its soldiers, as in
the "days" of 1830 and 1848, were the workers. The
ideology of the Commune was a mixture of neo-Jacobinism,
Proudhonism, and Blanquism, and each of these loosely
descriptive terms covers a multitude of political ideas.[28]

The role of the Blanquists in the Commune is known to
have been significant, but is also somewhat obscure and
subject to various interpretations. It is certain that the
Blanquists contributed a great deal to the consolidation of
the spontaneous rising that gave birth to the Commune.
They became the consistent supporters of vigorous direct
action against Versailles, and of many of the acts of violence
which marred the dying days of the Commune. The
Blanquists did not function as an organized political party
and confessed to a sense of confusion and lack of direction
which they felt the missing Blanqui would have supplied.

The Blanquists who did not perish in the final holocaust
fled abroad, especially to London. There they were somewhat influenced by Marxism, and supported Marx and
Engels in their struggle against the anarchists in the First
International. However, the Blanquists' exclusive devotion
to a program of immediate revolution alienated Marx
from them. A fear of Blanquist domination of the Inter-

28 Two relatively recent additions to the tremendous mass of literature on the Commune, which give well-reasoned but conflicting interpretations of its ideological composition are: E. S. Mason, *The Paris
Commune* (New York: MacMillan Co., 1930), and F. Jellinek, *The
Paris Commune of 1871* (London: Victor Gollanz Ltd., 1937).

national was probably one of Marx's motives for moving the headquarters of the organization to New York.[29]

While the Third Republic staggered through its first precarious years, Blanqui, the hero of a thousand battles for the republican ideal, remained behind the walls of a republican prison. In 1879 a campaign led by a group of young radicals resulted in Blanqui's election to the Chamber of Deputies by a Bordeaux constituency. The election was annulled by the Chamber which, at the same time, bowed to public opinion by giving him his liberty.[30] He became the editor of the newspaper *Ni Dieu Ni Maître,* and spent his last years stumping for a general amnesty of the Communards, and accusing the Opportunist republicans of a surrender to royalist and clerical forces. On December 27, 1880, he was felled by a stroke a few hours after speaking at a mass meeting in Paris. He died on January 1, 1881. His funeral was attended by a vast crowd of Parisian citizens, workers, and members of all leftist parties, for whom he had become the symbol of the long fight for socialism and for the Republic.[31]

After Blanqui's death his disciples tried to carry out his tradition in a "Blanquist" party, which eventually split over *Boulangisme* and was absorbed into the French Socialist Party.[32] Blanquism as the basis of a specific political party was dead, but its influence, direct and indirect, has been manifest in French leftist politics until today. As late as 1928 Albert Mathiez felt impelled to

29 F. Mehring, *Karl Marx* (New York: Covici-Friede, 1935), p. 511. This can only remain a conjecture, but the Blanquists would have been one of the strongest sections of an International purged of the anarchists if it had maintained its headquarters in London.

30 Geoffroy, *L'Enfermé,* II, 199.

31 *Ibid.,* II, 199.

32 Zévaès, *Auguste Blanqui,* pp. 232-46.

publish and refute Blanqui's previously unpublished critique of Robespierre, on the following grounds:

Blanqui exercised a very important influence on the *avant-garde* of the French revolutionary parties during nearly a half-century from 1830 to 1880. Although of delicate health, he outlived all of his rivals from Barbès to Proudhon and Raspail, who could have counterbalanced his popularity. With the prestige of a martyr's halo, he became, after the Commune, a sort of patriarch whose judgments were oracles. He had fanatic disciples who extended his influence long after his death, until the coming of Jaurès began to push it little by little into the shadows. The violent hate that Blanqui bore Robespierre has thus imposed a decisive deviation on the attitudes that the socialists held toward the founder of French democracy. They had adored him until 1848. Blanqui taught them to detest him.[33]

The persistence of Blanqui's influence in the French socialist movement is reflected in the controversy over Blanquism which disturbed the French Communist party a few years ago.[34]

Although Blanqui was committed to a predominantly French, one might say parochial, brand of socialism and had relatively little contact with the international revolutionary community of his era, his influence did pass beyond the borders of his beloved France. In 1848 the German socialist Lassalle pasted Blanqui's "Manifesto to the People" upon the door of his prison cell.[35] Sixty-seven years later Mussolini took from this same proclamation the phrase "He who has steel, has bread," for the masthead of his paper *Il Popolo d'Italia*.[36]

[33] A. Mathiez, "Notes de Blanqui sur Robespierre," *Annales Historiques de la Révolution Française*, V (July-Aug., 1928), 305-6.

[34] See p. 22 below.

[35] A. Schirokauer, *Lassalle,* tr. Edan and Cedar Paul (London: George Allen and Unwin Ltd., 1931), p. 124.

[36] G. Megaro, *Mussolini in the Making* (London: George Allen and Unwin Ltd., 1938), p. 324.

The link between Blanquism and Russian Bolshevism was embodied by Peter Tkatchev, a nineteenth-century revolutionary who was studied and admired by Lenin. Tkatchev was one of the first to introduce the idea of a vanguard revolutionary party and of a revolutionary dictatorship into Russian socialism.[37]   At Blanqui's funeral Tkatchev eulogized the Frenchman as a leader of the world revolutionary movement:

> To him, to his ideas, to his abnegation, to the clarity of his mind, to his clairvoyance, we owe in great measure the progress which daily manifests itself in the Russian revolutionary movement.
>
> Yes, it is he who has been our inspiration and our model in the great art of conspiracy. He is the uncontested chief who has filled us with revolutionary faith, the resolution to struggle, the scorn of suffering.[38]

THE MEANING OF THE LIFE

Many subsequent radicals, while rejecting Blanqui's political tactics, have found in his dedicated career the embodiment of the struggle to realize the idea of the Great Revolution in the nineteenth century.   Gustave Geffroy, the novelist and literary critic, who was a lifelong friend and journalistic collaborator of Clemenceau, wrote an impassioned tribute to Blanqui which is still the chief, albeit somewhat idealized, biography of the old revolutionary. He concluded this work with the observation: "Finally there is his life, which is itself a creation and his only doctrine—Blanqui was the political manifestation of the French Revolution in the nineteenth century." [39]

[37] M. Karpovitch, "A Forerunner of Lenin, P. N. Tkatchev," *Review of Politics*, IV (July, 1944), pp. 336-50.
[38] *Ni Dieu Ni Maître*, Jan. 9, 1881.
[39] Geffroy, *L'Enfermé*, II, 218-20.

In 1885, Benoît Malon, the integral socialist and firm supporter of eclectic and humanitarian reformism, wrote that Blanqui, lacking the personal attraction of Barbès, Mazzini, Garibaldi, or Bakunin, surpassed them all by the extent of his knowledge, the power of his mind, and "by the unity of his life, without a ray of personal pleasure, a life of suffering and struggle, for the emancipation of humanity." [40]

In 1920, Stalin contrasted the proletarian leaders who were men of action but weak in theory with theorists such as Plekhanov and Kautsky who contributed nothing to revolutionary practice. Blanqui was among the former, one of the "leaders in times of storm, practical leaders, self-sacrificing and courageous, but who were weak in theory." [41]

The almost universal agreement that Blanqui's career was a monument of indefatigable revolutionary purpose has not extended to his significance in the history of the socialist movement or to the substance of his social and political theory. The few lines assigned to Blanqui in histories of socialist thought usually characterize him as a naïve activist whose social theories are completely expressed in his career of abortive insurrections, candle-lit conspiracies, and perennial imprisonments.[42] He is often described as an anarchist [43] or terrorist who thought of social progress only in terms of barricade and bomb.

[40] B. Malon, "Blanqui Socialiste," *Revue Socialiste*, II (July, 1885), 597.

[41] J. Stalin, "Lenin as the Organizer and Leader of the Russian Communist Party," in Vol. I of V. I. Lenin, *Selected Works* (Moscow: Foreign Languages Publishing House, 1950), p. 34.

[42] For examples of this point of view: M. Prelot, *L'Évolution politique du socialisme français, 1789-1934* (Paris: Éditions Spes, 1939), p. 42; J. Plamenatz, *The Revolutionary Movement in France, 1815-71* (London: Longmans, Green and Co., 1952), p. 45.

[43] For example: D. Thomson, *Democracy in France* (London: Ox-

There has always been a minority, however, which finds in Blanqui's life something more than a series of revolutionary anecdotes and in his writings an important prevision of modern revolutionary socialism. The triumph of the Bolshevist brand of socialism has considerably increased the interest in Blanqui as a theorist. Both friendly and hostile critics of Bolshevism and Blanquism have called attention to the similarities between Blanqui's faith in a compact, disciplined, insurrectionist organization and the Leninist concept of a Communist elite which will act as the "advance guard" of the proletariat, as well as their common proclamation of the necessity for a revolutionary dictatorship over the disarmed bourgeoisie.[44]

The increasing interest in the possible relationship between Blanquism and contemporary ideologies has sharpened the controversy over the precise nature of Blanquism, especially in France where there is a very strong sense of the continuity between contemporary politics and its historical antecedents. Just as the heritage of the French Revolution or of the Commune of 1871 is claimed by the various publicists of the French left, each of whom finds his party the true heir of the French revolutionary tradition, so Blanqui, the personification of that tradition throughout the nineteenth century is retroactively enlisted in the ranks of the various factions. French political groupings, from the Radical Socialists to the Stalinists, have found something in Blanqui which is a reflection of their own ideologies, which they consider characteristic of all that is

ford University Press, 1946), p. 25. "Blanqui represents the simplest form of the revolutionary tradition, anti-parlimentarian and anarchist . . ."

44 E. Mason, "Blanqui and Communism," *Political Science Quarterly*, XLIV (Dec., 1929), 498. R. W. Postgate, "The Prisoner," *Out of the Past* (London: The Labour Publishing Co. Ltd., 1922), p. 54.

praiseworthy in Blanquism. They all distinguish between Blanquist errors and the true inheritance which has been passed to them alone.

Some of Blanqui's greatest admirers have denied that he exhibited any theoretical capacity whatsoever. Georges Clemenceau, who was a Blanquist in his youth, described his old master as virtually a democratic saint,[45] but so completely a man of action as to be a total stranger to systematic thought.[46] The great Radical Socialist politician was proud of his association with the old revolutionary and identified himself and his party with Blanqui's struggle against the nineteenth-century monarchies. Yet when one considers Clemenceau's career it seems obvious that the man who came to be such an enemy of revolutionary socialism must be considered not the heir, but the antithesis of Blanqui, unless the latter's expression of revolutionary and socialist values is completely discounted and only his qualities of leadership and disinterestedness are considered characteristic.

Benoît Malon, on the other hand, placed Blanquism in an essential relationship to late nineteenth-century socialism: "Blanqui's work gives us a sort of synthesis of Babouvist revolutionism and scientific socialism." [47] This viewpoint has been expressed even more strongly by some modern French historians and socialists. For example, Maurice Dommanget, the outstanding contemporary biographer of Blanqui, not only credits him with a valid and

[45] Clemenceau wrote a brief eulogy of Blanqui in *Le Journal,* Nov. 27, 1896.

[46] Sylvain Molinier described a conversation with Clemenceau in which he expressed this viewpoint. S. Molinier, *Blanqui* (Paris: Presses Universitaires de France, 1948), p. 69.

[47] B. Malon, "Blanqui Socialiste," *Revue Socialiste,* II (July, 1885), 597.

clearly formulated social theory, but sees in his writings a brilliant theoretical edifice which in many ways is a precursor of Marxism and actually is congruent with it in all essentials.   Dommanget flatly states,

the liaison between Babouvism and Bolshevism by way of revolutionary Marxism is realized, so to speak, through Blanquism. . . . Blanqui formulated, in nearly the same terms as Marx, the law of accumulation.[48]

The relation of Blanquist theory to Marxism has been the subject of continuous interpretation by Marxists ever since Marx himself in 1852 described Blanqui and his followers as "the real leaders of the proletarian party, the revolutionary communists." [49]   Subsequently Blanquism has been the subject of rigorous criticism and moderate praise by Engels,[50] Lenin,[51] and Stalin, and of course of special interest to French Communists.   In 1951 a Parisian Society of the Friends of Blanqui was formed which opened its proceedings with an address entitled "Some Aspects of Blanqui's Activity" by André Marty, at that time still one of the leaders of the French Communist party.[52]   In this

[48] M. Dommanget, *Auguste Blanqui à Belle-Ile,* pp. 7-11.

[49] K. Marx, "The Eighteenth Brumaire of Louis Bonaparte," *Selected Works,* ed. V. Adoratsky (New York: International Publishers, 1939), II, 323.

[50] For Engels's critique of Blanquism see his letter to *Der Volksstaat,* 1874, No. 73; "The Program of the Blanquist Fugitives from the Paris Commune," reprinted in K. Marx, *The Civil War in France* (Chicago: Charles H. Kerr and Co., 1934), pp. 133-44.   There is also an interesting remark of Engels's to the effect that Russia was the only country in which a Blanquist conspiracy might succeed, in "A letter to Vera Zasulich, April 23, 1885," reprinted in Marx-Engels, *Selected Correspondence,* Vol. XXIX of *Marxist Library* (New York: International Publishers, 1942), p. 437.

[51] For Lenin's distinction between Blanquism and Bolshevism see: V. I. Lenin, *On the Eve of October,* Vol. XIII of *Little Lenin Library* (New York: International Publishers, 1932), pp. 5, 41.

[52] A. Marty, *Quelques Aspects de l'activité de Blanqui* (Paris: So-

pamphlet Blanqui was given a position of considerable importance as a forerunner of modern Marxism-Leninism. Marty asserted that Blanqui's political role had been distorted by "bourgeois and social-democrat" historians who minimized his positive contributions and maximized his errors. Communists should realize that Blanqui is to be praised for his clear conception of the class struggle and its consequence, the bitter fight against the middle class, the instrument of capitalist domination of the workers. At the same time the two great Blanquist errors, the lack of interest in agitation for the workers' everyday economic demands, and the absence of any scientific conception of revolution, should be discussed as lessons for modern young revolutionaries and workers.

Marty himself was subsequently accused by the French Communist party of a lack of faith in the masses which has led him to attempt the substitution of "a narrow and sectarian Blanquist conception" for the Leninist-Stalinist idea of a party "immersed in the working class and the masses." [53]

Marty's political sins include an apparent scorn for mass propaganda efforts, such as the Stockholm peace petition; the heretical insistence that, in 1944, the Communists could have seized power in France; and "factionalist maneuvers" which are marked by covert demonstrations of hostility toward Maurice Thorez. An article in the January, 1953, issue of *Cahiers du Communisme,* the organ of the Central Committee of the French Communist party,

---

ciété des Amis de Blanqui, 1951). This also appeared in: *Cahiers du Communisme,* April, 1951, pp. 389-415.

[53] Le Bureau Politique du Parti Communiste Français, "Les problèmes de la politique du parti, et l'activité factionelle des camarades André Marty et Charles Tillon," *Cahiers du Communisme,* Oct., 1952, p. 951.

attacked Marty's brochure on Blanqui as the theoretical manifestation of his opposition to the will of the party and to Leninist principles.   According to the Communist historian Roger Garaudy, Marty has mistakenly credited Blanqui with a clear formulation of the class struggle; he has ignored Blanqui's essentially *petit bourgeois* economic ideas; and he has dismissed without sufficient criticism Blanqui's idealist interpretation of progress and historical development.   Under the cover of Blanqui's well-deserved prestige he has attempted to smuggle "neo-Blanquist" errors of adventurism, nationalism, and factionalism into the organization.[54]

The very elements of Blanquism which modern Communists do praise, such as the insistence upon a vanguard organization of professional revolutionaries and a post-revolutionary dictatorship, are often characterized by anti-Bolsheviks as Leninist perversions of true Marxism.   In K. J. Kenafick's work on Marx and Bakunin, which has a definite anarchist orientation, Leninism is defined as "Marxism plus Blanquism" and the present Russian dictatorship is described as essentially Blanquist: "for it is based on the conception of a 'vanguard party,' a party of ruthless and violent action, and this is a Blanquist, and not a Marxist conception." [55]

Max Eastman, in his *Marx and Lenin,* remarked that Lenin "corrected the error of Blanqui which was to trust all to the organization of revolutionists," but asserted that Lenin's insistence on centralized authority and military discipline in the party which leads the proletariat "smacks

[54] R. Garaudy, "Le Néo-blanquisme de contrebande et les positions antiléninistes d'André Marty," *Cahiers du Communisme,* Jan., 1953, pp. 38-50.

[55] K. J. Kenafick, *Michael Bakunin and Karl Marx* (Melbourne: Hawthorn Press, 1948), pp. 276-77.

more of the tactics of Blanqui than of the philosophy of Marx." [56]

Communists have praised and anticommunists have criticized Blanqui's alleged uncompromising militancy and revolutionary authoritarianism. However, the image of Blanqui as activist and relentless conspirator is not the only one.[57] Many French socialists and republicans have interpreted his statements, especially those on education and universal suffrage, as fundamentally reformist. They argue that in the reactionary France of 1815-1871, a revolution was perhaps the only meaningful expression of political dissent for a sincere and selfless reformer. In a republic, even a bourgeois republic, which permitted freedom of speech, association, and the press, Blanqui would have eschewed conspiratorial techniques and carried on his fight through the press, the tribune, and the ballot box. The last two years of his life, in which he criticized the leaders of the Third Republic without attempting to overthrow its institutions are cited as evidence of his fundamentally reformist position. Therefore many parliamentarians and moderate reformers have accepted Blanqui's revolutionary career as a worthy contribution to the glorious French Republican tradition, while characterizing their own nonrevolutionary position as a logical consequence of his ideas, applied in a different milieu.

In the *Encyclopédie Socialiste* of 1912, Compère-Morel affirmed Blanqui's revolutionism, but listed the bases of Blanquism as *"Liberté, Laïcité, Instruction:* These are the

[56] M. Eastman, *Marx and Lenin* (New York: Albert and Charles Boni, 1927), pp. 144-45.

[57] A. Rosenberg, *Democracy and Socialism,* tr. G. Roben (New York: Alfred A. Knopf, 1939), p. 94: "Blanqui was neither a fomenter of insurrections, nor an adventurer. Instead he was the living conscience of French democracy."

three ideas behind Blanqui's action.   Communism will result from them quite naturally." [58]   Social Democrats have quoted this analysis out of context to prove that Blanqui was essentially a democratic reformer whose primary commitment was to universal secular education.[59] One republican anticlerical went so far as to maintain that in his last hours Blanqui saw the reversal of his belief in the necessity of violent revolution and the imminent solution of *all* social problems by the application of the new anticlerical laws.[60]

Blanqui's fiery patriotism has often been cited as the truly French radical's answer to socialist pacifism or revolutionary internationalism.   During the First World War especially, Blanqui's fierce anti-German polemics were exhumed and used to identify him as a spiritual forebear of Clemenceau's fighting nationalism, and as the antithesis of Marxian internationalism.[61]   On the other hand, in at least one speech delivered during a period when French socialism was strongly internationalist and pacifist, the lesson of Blanqui's life was found to be "a call to the fight against religion, capitalism, and patriotism." [62]

It is apparent that the essential nature of Blanquism, which seems so obviously embodied in Blanqui's singularly unified political experience, has been interpreted according

[58] C. Rappaport and Compère-Morel, *Un Peu d'histoire,* Vol. I of *Encyclopédie Socialiste,* ed. Compère-Morel (Paris: Aristide Quillet, 1912), p. 291.

[59] Cf. F. Simon, *L. A. Blanqui en Anjou,* (Angers: Cooperative Imprimerie Angevine, 1939), pp. 51-54.

[60] Sénés, "Blanqui," in *Provenceaux—Notes Biographiques* (Toulon, 1904), p. 146.

[61] E.g., A. Callet "Un Grand patriote méconnu. Auguste Blanqui," *La Nouvelle Revue,* XXXV (May-June 1918), 111-18.

[62] E. Albringues, *Discours anniversaire de Blanqui,* aux Jeunesse Socialiste Révolutionnaire, Groupe de Toulouse, Jan. 1, 1898 (Toulouse: Imprimerie Lagout et Sebille, 1898), p. 8.

to various predispositions, each of which can be supported by some relevant quotation from Blanqui's writings. Therefore Blanqui can, to some extent, be placed in a correct historical perspective by an analysis of the total content of his expressed ideas, the premises from which they were derived, and the historical context in which they were formulated. An understanding must be sought, not in the so-called "Blanquism" of his disciples, nor solely in the dramatic events of his crowded political career, but in the text of his own writings and speeches as well.

Unfortunately, not everything that Blanqui wrote has been preserved. His published writings make up only a segment of his intellectual output and actually give an incomplete and distorted impression of his total viewpoint. The bulk of his salvaged unpublished manuscripts is bound in twenty volumes in the Paris Bibliothèque Nationale.[63] From this disorganized mass of notes, letters, and drafts for speeches and pamphlets, from fragments which have been collected in his published works, and from the speeches he made at his various trials, one can piece together the outline of a social and political philosophy.

This material demonstrated, first of all, that Blanqui, "the activist," was a self-conscious intellectual and omnivorous reader, interested in theoretical formulations of innumerable social, scientific, and philosophic problems. Among his notes are thousands of abstracts of books and periodical articles, often followed by his own comments. He read widely not only in contemporary political problems, but in the histories of every period, geographies, books

[63] Bibliothèque Nationale, Blanqui MSS, Nouvelles acquisitions françaises, 9578-9598. (Will henceforth be cited as Blanqui MSS, followed by Nouvelles acquisitions number, section, and page, e.g., Blanqui MSS, 9580 [part 2], p. 33).

on military science, collections of national population and economic statistics, philosophic treatises, and scientific articles of every description. His interests ranged from techniques for pressing grapes to the problem of the limits of the universe, and from the history of the early church fathers to the population statistics of Illinois.[64]

This extensive intellectual preparation was to furnish the material for Blanqui's discursive theorizing which usually took the form of trenchant but rather unsystematic polemics written to define and defend the role of revolutionary socialism in France. Some of these ideas are now commonplace and so directly related to action that they are not usually dignified with the label of "theory." Nevertheless a theory of action has as much instructive content as a carefully constructed Utopia, and a somewhat greater relevance to contemporary social movements.

Blanqui, the man of action *par excellence,* perfectly exemplified the fact that all political action, rational or irrational, is connected with certain ideas, unconscious or explicit, about reality, man, and society. Without an understanding of "Blanquist" theory, a full assessment of Blanqui's historical role in the socialist movement cannot be made.

[64] This is attested by various fellow prisoners: Noguès, *Une Condamnation de Mai 1839*, p. 242; A. Scheurer-Kestner, *Souvenirs de jeunesse* (Paris: Bibliothèque—Charpentier, 1905), pp. 80-81.

CHAPTER TWO

The Philosophic Foundations of Blanquism

IN THE POPULAR mind, politics and philosophy are antithetical. Presumably, the political world is one of vigorous and purposeful action in which avowed altruism is usually perverted by personal and class ambitions. The philosopher, on the other hand, pursues his disinterested quest for truth in a world of quiet contemplation, disassociated from the everyday sufferings and needs of men.

Yet upon reflection it should be easy to grasp the historical importance of the relationship between so-called "abstract" ideas and political action. Not only are all political creeds based either consciously or implicitly on assumptions of knowledge, being, and human nature, but philosophers consciously fashion ideological ammunition for the conflicts of class and party. The devastating volleys of Voltaire are answered by the batteries of Burke and De Maistre.

In the nineteenth century, political leaders themselves were forced again and again to erect and defend a philosophic system in order to establish the validity of their political programs. In modern radical politics, and especially in the struggles about, against, and around Marxism, a continuous and bitter polemic over the most abstract philosophic concepts has gone hand in hand with conflicts in the political sphere. Driven by similar motives and influences Blanqui made an effort to erect a philosophic foundation and buttress for his political values, which he knew would be subjected to the probing assault of a host of enemies.

As is often the case, Blanqui's political nonconformism was prior to, and to some degree a cause of, his iconoclastic philosophy. In his earliest letters and political writings we find him calling on the will of God [1] and referring respectfully to the connection between *Égalité* and the first principles of Christianity,[2] but in the course of his personal war against the values and institutions of his society, he developed an outright position of combative atheism resting on the tradition of philosophic materialism. With the belief that organized religion and the very idea of "God" were the source of all social evil [3] came the insistence that the reformer must carry his social struggle into the field of metaphysics. Philosophy's first task must be the resolution of the supreme problems, those of human destiny and social morality, which it could accomplish if it were to base itself upon science and experience instead of upon those superstitious hypotheses which inevitably gave birth to error.[4]

For Blanqui the philosophic truths which are apprehended by scientific observation and which are mighty weapons in the struggle against clerical obscurantism are based squarely upon the work of the great teachers of materialism. He criticized Comte for his "bad faith" in praising only the Deist rationalists of the eighteenth century and ignoring the "materialist pleiades" of Diderot,

---

[1] Letters of Blanqui to Mlle Montgolfier, Aug. 5, 1831, and Feb. 12, 1834, in *Les Lettres,* Première Anneé, VIII (Sept. 6, 1906), pp. 509, 519.

[2] Excerpt from Blanqui's newspaper *Le Libérateur* of Feb. 2, 1834. Copied by Blanqui in his manuscripts: Blanqui MSS, 9592 (part 3), pp. 4-5.

[3] Blanqui in his newspaper *Ni Dieu Ni Maître,* Nov. 6, 1881.

[4] Blanqui MSS, 9591 (part 1), p. 388.

D'Holbach, D'Alembert, and De la Mettrie.[5]   As for true socialists, they would take their stand "in the school inaugurated in the eighteenth century by Diderot and D'Holbach and sanctioned in the nineteenth century by the verdict of science." [6]

Just how strongly Blanqui was committed to this tradition is indicated in his list of the "liberators of the human intellect."   The list reads: "Diagoras, Democritus, Aristotle, Zeno, Epicurus, Epictetus, Lucretius, Pliny the Elder, Marcus Aurelius, Spinoza, Diderot, D'Holbach, Helvétius, D'Alembert, Cabanis, Broussais, Laplace, Lalande, Feuerbach, etc." [7]

Here, beside the pioneers of atheist materialism are listed the great empirics and rationalists—all, in some measure, devoted to the conception of a knowable universe in which power and knowledge are the fruits of reason.   Also, the significance of Blanqui's classical education and his narrowly French intellectual orientation is clearly exemplified by the list.   He was, however, aware of the ideas of contemporary foreign materialists, especially Feuerbach and the German mechanists, Vogt, Moleschott, and Buchner.[8]

Blanqui himself scarcely bothered to formulate the basic epistemological premise of a materialist philosophy.   He obviously assumed that there was an objective, knowable universe in existence prior to mind or idea.   This can be seen in his characterization of "Nature" as a term representing the universe of incessantly moving matter [9] and his statement that matter neither evolved from nothingness

[5] *Ibid.*, 9590 (part 1), p. 66.
[6] *Ibid.*, 9591 (part 2), p. 373.
[7] *Ni Dieu Ni Maître*, Nov. 27, 1880.
[8] Blanqui MSS, 9587, p. 437.
[9] *Ibid.*, 9591 (part 2), p. 353.

nor will become nothingness—that it is eternal and imperishable.[10]

The militant atheist identified all criticism of a materialist metaphysic with *spiritualisme,* which, for him, meant all religious doctrine or any intellectual compromise with the pressures of organized religion. Pantheistic theories, for example, represent timid efforts to substitute the idea of an impersonal God for the anthropomorphism which makes God a gigantic caricature of man. In everyday language and for all practical religious purposes the word "God" implies personality. Therefore pantheism is in practice no different from atheism except that it has disguised its negation of God by timid sophistry and equivocation.[11]

Of much greater contemporary interest is Blanqui's critique of positivist scepticism. Blanqui had been raised in the tradition which saw in each increment of scientific knowledge a blow against the massed forces of ignorance and prejudice, and, by extension, against political and religious oppression. In the nineteenth century, philosophers of science, of whom Comte was perhaps the most notable, began to posit scientific theories which continued to envision the scientific reconstruction of society but which carried conservative, or at least neutral, political implications. Comte himself derived extremely conservative, not to say totalitarian, conclusions from his structure of "positive" science. Many of his disciples, rejecting the reactionary and religious paraphernalia of the master arrived at a sceptical and "objective" attitude toward nature and society which has been the hallmark of positivism ever since.

---

[10] L. A. Blanqui, *L'Éternité par les astres* (Paris: Librairie Germer Baillière, 1872), p. 6.

[11] Blanqui MSS, 9587, p. 341.

In the nineteenth century began a dispute between positivism and materialism which often contained political implications. Philosophic controversy on the political left especially has often centered around these issues. From the polemics of Engels against the Humeans and Kantians [12] through Lenin's attack on the neo-positivism of Mach and Avenarius [13] to the recent Communist criticisms of logical positivism and related theories,[14] orthodox Marxists have again and again attempted to purge proletarian philosophy of what they consider a heretical deviation from Marx's positive affirmation of the reality and priority of the material universe. Blanqui's quarrel with the disciples of Comte adumbrated the fundamental position which the dialectical materialists have since taken in their struggle against sceptical or "neutralist" theories of reality.

Blanqui admitted the real value of many of the "materialist" investigations of the Comtists but described their refusal to make any metaphysical statement about the existence of matter as philosophically incorrect.[15] Their scepticism was a system of consistent doubt carried out to the absurd point at which doubt itself became a religion whose true characteristics were negativism and nihilism, not "Positivism." [16] Characteristically, it is the positivists' neutrality in regard to religion which is the target of

[12] F. Engels, *Ludwig Feuerbach—and the Outcome of Classical German Philosophy*, Vol. XV of *Marxist Library*, *Works of Marxism-Leninism* (New York: International Publishers, n.d.), pp. 34-35.

[13] V. I. Lenin, *Materialism and Empirico-Criticism*, Vol. XIII of *Collected Works of V. I. Lenin* (New York: International Publishers, 1927), *passim*.

[14] D. Guest, *A Textbook of Dialectical Materialism* (New York: International Publishers, 1939), p. 30. The author, referring to the ideas of Bertrand Russell writes: "This line of argument which starts with 'philosophic doubt' is truly self-destructive."

[15] Blanqui MSS, 9590 (part 1), p. 65.

[16] *Ibid.*, p. 60.

Blanqui's most forceful denunciations. Their abstention from metaphysics actually leaves the field to Christianity, and thus a misguided or affected respect for science may deliver science into the hands of its greatest enemy. Besides, a scepticism which is neutral on the question of the existence of God is invalid. There is no refuge for this idea in some untouchable metaphysical realm, for it has already been judged and found wanting by "Mathematics and Physiology." [17] Long before the vaunted revelation of Comte's "Positive Science" men had begun to grasp the truths of atheism and materialism through their experience of the real world.[18] The reason for the positivists' refusal to face the materialist consequences of their position is cowardice [19] in the face of social and political pressure. In fact it is impossible to "ignore political influences and to imagine that thought depends upon itself alone and never upon exterior pressures." [20]

In these scattered criticisms of the Comtists Blanqui was not primarily concerned with the formulation of abstract epistemological truths, but with combating influential ideas which carried what he considered to be unhealthy political consequences. The implications of his approach to the philosophy of knowledge and being are contained in many modern philosophies of political radicalism: it is through common-sense experience and the daily gains of empirical science that our unassailable knowledge of material reality is derived. The evaluation of a philosophy must include an estimate of its social context and its political consequences. The assertion "whoever is not with us is against us" has its philosophic as well as its political application.

17 Blanqui MSS, 9592 (part 1), pp. 118-19.
18 *Ibid.*, 9590 (part 1), pp. 176-77.
19 *Ni Dieu Ni Maître*, Dec. 19, 1880.
20 Blanqui MSS, 9592 (part 1), pp. 162-63.

The more theoretical aspects of Blanqui's philosophy follow (more or less consistently) one standard materialist approach.   He defined matter as merely the *ensemble de ses propriétés* and, like Lenin,[21] insisted that any concept of an underlying substance or substratum is only a metaphysical absurdity.[22]   However, all forms of matter are transitory,[23] and the discernible effects of matter—that is, "heat, light, and motion"—are its discernible forces but are not themselves matter.[24]

In an apparent attempt to define matter without falling into the metaphysical traps which the problems of its subjective apprehension entail, Blanqui merely affirms a number of tautologies which tell us nothing more about matter than that it exists.   He implicitly rests his case, as almost all materialists ultimately do, upon the universal commonsense apprehension of a real external world.

Although there is a passage in his notes (dated 1869) in which Blanqui without any further explanation referred to the "nonsense of atomism," [25] his cosmography, which is set out in his pseudoscientific work, *L'Éternité par les astres* (1872), is largely based upon an atomic theory of matter and motion.   This odd little causerie on astronomy and the composition of the universe was the last fruit produced through the "perpetual prisoner's" painfully developed technique of spiritual escape from the deadening pressure of physical confinement.   In the miserable cell of a lonely island fortress where the government of Thiers left him and under the closest and most harassing supervision, Blanqui tried to lift himself out of his surroundings by

---

[21] Lenin, *Materialism and Emperico-Criticism*, p. 222.
[22] Blanqui MSS, 9592 (part 3), p. 223 (dated 1868).
[23] Blanqui, *L'Éternité par les astres*, p. 33.
[24] *Ibid.*, p. 39.
[25] Blanqui MSS, 9590 (part 1), p. 155.

contemplating the heavens and the problems of the infinite extension of time and space.[26] The result, surprising to those who knew Blanqui only as a political activist, was a well-written potpourri of elementary science, philosophic insights, and outlandish hypotheses. Although his flights of astronomical fancy contribute nothing to the progress of scientific thought, they embody the assumptions upon which rests his philosophy of being and change.

The pamphlet begins with a characterization of the universe as "infinite in time and space, eternal, without limits, and indivisible." [27] The infinity of space is peopled by an infinite number of incessantly moving bodies which comprise not only the universe in its entirety but "all of the forms of matter, even the infusoria and the grain of sand." [28] The universal motion caused by the great *force fécondatrice* of attraction (i.e., gravity) is manifested to us by light and heat and is the source of the energy of the universe.[29] In this motion lies the answer to problems which the astronomers have been unable to solve.

According to Blanqui, even Laplace, from whom he drew most of his astronomical ideas, had never come to grips with the problem of the birth and death of stars in a universe where the laws of entropy should have inevitably resulted in an infinity of cold, lifeless worlds.[30] Blanqui's solution lay in the incessant motion of astral bodies and in the fact that occasional "mutations" of physical laws occur which permit a dead star to leave its orbit.[31] In its anarchistic flight across the heavens it may collide with some other giant astral body and in this mutual destruction generate the heat which forms those whirling balls of fire which are

26 G. Geffroy, *L'Enfermé*, II, 155-56.
27 Blanqui, *L'Éternité par les astres*, p. 5.
28 *Ibid.*, p. 70.   29 *Ibid.*, p. 40.
30 *Ibid.*, p. 28.   31 *Ibid.*, p. 41.

the new stars.[32]   This explanation, admits Blanqui, satisfies all logical requirements but is still provisional at best.

A consequence of a cosmography of incessant motion is the concept of infinite change, yet for Blanqui there was a limit to the modes of existence which people the universe. He had been impressed by the results of spectrum analysis which seemed to demonstrate the universal existence of a limited number of basic elements.   The possible number of combinations of these elements, no matter how large, was finite.   Therefore an infinity of matter was composed of an infinite repetition of a limited number of combinations or forms.[33]

The conception of the endless repetition of every possible mode of existence led Blanqui to a conclusion, which he may have borrowed from Epicurus,[34] to the effect that every event which has occurred on earth is being endlessly repeated in some other solar system, and that everything which could possibly have occurred on our planet, but has not, must have taken place on some other world.   Blanqui stated this problem not as a logical possibility but as a categorical necessity, and evoked worlds in other solar systems where Grouchy had not blundered and the battle of Waterloo was won, as well as worlds, in all fairness, where Napoleon had perhaps tasted defeat at some less happy Marengo.[35]

Notwithstanding the obvious logical aberrations concerning repetitions of earthly life on other worlds, many contemporaries were impressed by Blanqui's grasp and ex-

32 *Ibid.,* p. 33.

33 *Ibid.,* p. 46-47.

34 F. A. Lange, *The History of Materialism* (New York: Harcourt, Brace and Co., 1925), I, 151.

35 Blanqui, *L'Éternité par les astres,* p. 57.

position of modern science.[36]   There can be little doubt
that Blanqui had a fairly sophisticated knowledge of recent advances in the physical sciences; yet he devoted a
large portion of the pamphlet to a very simple description
of the basic principles of chemistry and astronomy.   The
usual estimate of *L'Éternité par les astres* as a well-written
cosmological romance (which carried the old prisoner out
of his mundane sufferings) does not quite explain the
didactic and expository portions of the work. Perhaps the
"enlightened" Paris worker, the hero of all Blanqui's
dreams of revolution, was seen as a potential public for
this seemingly nonpolitical work.   Education and political
action are inseparably joined in Blanqui's mind, so that a
great deal of the work can be plausibly explained as an
effort to present, in very elementary terms, a series of ideas
on the immensities of space and the relative insignificance
of man which have from time to time shaken the religious
faith of even the strongest believers.   Even the indirect inculcation of antireligious attitudes would for Blanqui have
fulfilled one of the highest political functions.

The arguments of the pamphlet are lucidly and persua-
sively presented, but they betray Blanqui's most characteristic intellectual weakness.   Most simply, this was the old
rationalist complaint of excessive faith in deduction.
Throughout his writings one discovers the assumption that
the most reasonable of a set of provisional hypotheses has
the force of an empirically established proposition.   In his
ruminations upon astronomy Blanqui stated with complete assurance that the comets (the nature of which was at
that time an astronomical mystery) were composed of an
indefinable, perfectly translucent substance which was

[36] See *République Française*, March 18, 1872; *Opinion Nationale*,
March 25, 1872.

neither liquid, solid, nor gas, but some mode of existence entirely unlike anything else in the universe.[37]

In *L'Éternité par les astres* is Blanqui's most vigorous expression of the classic rationalist belief in the immanence of law in nature. The relation of nature to physical laws was sometimes expressed in terms borrowed directly from the naïve anthropomorphism of the seventeenth and eighteenth centuries. In the year 1872 he was still able to praise "Nature's" skill in adapting organisms to their milieux without ever swerving "from a general plan which dominates all its works." [38]   He once predicted that balloons could never be successfully steered, because man can do no more than imitate Nature, and a self-directing creature lighter than air would long since have been evolved by Nature if it had been compatible with Nature's laws.[39]

It was, however, too late in the nineteenth century for Blanqui, who was cognizant of the main currents of contemporary science and philosophy, to maintain consistently the image of the "world machine." He checked his paean to the inexorable workings of Nature to warn the reader that the universe is in no way analogous to a clock,[40] and even to deny any attributes of morality or purpose to Nature which merely "with closed eyes applies the calculus of probabilities better than all of the mathematicians can explain it with their eyes wide open." [41]

Finally, with an apparent bow in the direction of Hegelianism, he concluded *L'Éternité par les astres* by delineating the universe in purely nonmechanistic terms:

[37] Blanqui, *L'Éternité par les astres*, pp. 26-27.
[38] *Ibid.*, p. 11.
[39] Blanqui MSS, 9587, p. 340.
[40] Blanqui, *L'Éternité par les astres*, p. 33.
[41] *Ibid.*, p. 67.

The universe is at the same time life and death, destruction and creation, change and stability, tumult and repose . . . it is a perpetual becoming. . . . In its whole and its parts it is eternally transformation and immanence.[42]

Perhaps Blanqui's idea of Nature and natural law is best expressed in his characterization of "Nature" as no more than a word for eternal universal law.[43]

Blanqui's picture of the universe would seem to imply a completely determinist philosophy. In fact the vision of endless worlds which endlessly reproduce all possible events appears to prohibit anything indeterminate, especially since Blanqui insists that no mutations can spontaneously arise out of matter. For instance: "the initial movements of a star determine the entire series of its material transformation." [44]   At this point, however, Blanqui introduces a "but" which is of tremendous significance for his entire social and political philosophy. "But," he says, "the variations begin with animated beings which have wills, that is to say caprices . . . above all wherever men appear, fantasy appears with them." [45]   Furthermore the concept of "law" applies only to physical nature and not to the human will.[46]

With these phrases, Blanqui turned his back on what many consider the essence or necessary consequence of materialism. Bertrand Russell describes the assertion of the "reign of law" as a fundamental materialist dogma and one which can only be consistently materialist when law is believed "to have no exceptions, not even human volitions." [47]

42 Blanqui, *L'Éternité par les astres*, p. 72.
43 Blanqui MSS, 9587, p. 341.
44 Blanqui, *L'Éternité par les astres*, p. 63.
45 *Ibid.*
46 Blanqui MSS, 9590 (part 1), p. 278.
47 In Russell's introduction to F. A. Lange, *History of Materialism*, I, xii-xiii.

Blanqui had to reconcile his introduction of human caprice and conscious choice with his insistence that the "metaphysical entity, free will," did not exist [48] and that "No matter what choice one makes one cannot escape fatality." [49]   His attempt to resolve the paradox must be sought in his theory of the human mind and its relation to the body and the social environment.   One is not surprised to discover a series of statements on the relationship of mind to brain which are characteristic expressions of forthright mechanistic monism.   Blanqui several times identified himself with the ideas of Cabanis and borrowed Cabanis's famous descriptions of "thought" as a secretion of the brain.[50]   He eventually modified this concept in the light of nineteenth-century science.   Thought was indeed a faculty or "special property" of the brain activated by sensations received from the outer world.[51]   However, it was not precisely a secretion, but rather a sort of electrical emission, an effect of the combined action of heat and electricity.[52]

An obvious consequence of this observation, and a weapon for Blanqui's persistent atheist propaganda, was the rejection of any concept of personality or self as distinct from the total of cerebral activities.   There can be no "I" independent of the brain: "The self is uniquely a property of the organism, destined to disappear with it." [53] This apparently rigorous behavorism is rounded out by several passages asserting that man is but a higher animal

48 Blanqui MSS, 9592 (part 1), p. 263.
49 Blanqui L'Éternité par les astres, p. 57.
50 Blanqui MSS, 9587, p. 410 (dated 1863).
51 Ibid., 9592 (part 1), p. 263.
52 Ibid., 9590 (part 1), p. 25 (dated 1868).   He was probably influenced by Broussais, a physician who popularized the conception of mind as a purely physiological phenomenon.
53 Ibid., p. 177.

and that ideas of human immortality are only desperate efforts to obscure the essential identity of man and beast.[54] The passages cited are familiar aspects of a standard behaviorist and mechanistic interpretation of the Mind-Body interaction which was exposited in the eighteenth century by De la Mettrie and D'Holbach, and, in the nineteenth, by the German physiologists Moleschott, Vogt, and Buchner.

The reconciliation of these ideas with Blanqui's introduction of "human caprice" into an otherwise determinate cosmos would appear to present a formidable problem. Indeed, Blanqui's lifelong commitment to social change by the volition of dedicated individuals must be seriously challenged by a completely mechanistic conception of human behavior. How could he carry on his opposition to the positivist acceptance of an inevitable past and an inexorable future if he himself believed that mental states are merely a series of electrochemical, hence analyzable and predictable, reactions? Blanqui was very conscious of the paradox and approached the problem in a series of propositions which to some degree parallel the position of the dialectical materialists.

Some of his ideas can only be considered as an unconscious attempt to allow dualism to enter a monistic theory by the back door. There is, for example, an obvious separation of matter from mind in his characterization of "Nature" as "active matter, which gives us 'thought' which she does not have herself and does not need." [55] However, Blanqui does establish a more consistent line of investigation in his analysis of the relationship between the human brain and its environment. His conclusions were em-

54 *Ibid.*, 9581, p. 371.
55 *Ibid.*, 9591 (part 2), p. 353.

bodied in the dialectical aphorism: "The brain makes the man, but the man also makes the brain." [56]

According to Blanqui, thought was indeed a product of "a nervous substance" and varied according to its modifications, but the substance itself—that is, the brain—could in turn be modified by its own product, the mind. Here lay man's ability to effect his own destiny—and, in fact, the successes of humanity have been proportional to the "reaction of thought upon the cerebral organism." [57] Specifically, the brain, like a muscle, can be changed by exercise —that is, thought—and the change can be genetically transmitted. Thus the very physical structure of the brain can, in the course of generations, be insensibly transformed by the continuous "influence" of thought.[58]

The gradual development of the idea of "human solidarity" is given as an example. At first, man loved only his immediate family, but as he perceived the value of the assistance of his fellow man, an apprehension of solidarity grew in his brain until it attained *l'état d'instinct* finally to be transmitted from generation to generation.[59] Blanqui felt that he was merely carrying out a logical extension of Darwinism,[60] but it would appear that he was actually substituting for the principle of selection that of the inheritance of acquired characteristics.

He eventually decided that the passage of centuries might not be necessary for a fundamental cerebral transformation. The life span of a single man might suffice. It was true, he admitted, that changes in individual ideas do not reflect complete change in the basic constitution of the brain which contains the potentialities of all of an individual's possible acts and ideas. Through environment,

56 *Ibid.*, 9592 (part 1), p. 270.
57 *Ibid.*, 9592 (part 1), p. 241.   58 *Ibid.*, p. 275.
59 *Ibid.*, pp. 271-72.   60 *Ibid.*, pp. 276.

however—and Blanqui specifically had education in mind—
certain cerebral tendencies can be nourished and others
atrophied so that in the course of a human life a basic
mental transformation will have occurred.[61]   The product
of these transformations—that is, ideas—in turn could af-
fect and improve society: "The perfecting of brain and
civilization are equally cause and effect in the successive
transformation. . . ." [62]

With these qualifications of a purely mechanistic materialism, Blanqui attempts to fashion a philosophy for political action.   It is by establishing the reciprocity of will
and environment that he hopes to escape the dilemma of
the positivists who had been unable "to reconcile the ir-
reconcilables of social development following its necessary
course, and the intervention of human intelligence." [63]

According to Blanqui, Comtists such as Littré have espoused a Moslem fatalism which led them to a doctrine of
inevitable progress and to a life of apologetics and political
resignation.[64]   If one accepts their position, one does not,
for example, warn the workers away from political error,
one merely intervenes magisterially after the fact with the
information that it had been infallibly determined.   The
dedicated revolutionary must insist that an event such as the
Eighteenth Brumaire was neither progress nor infallible
necessity, but an avoidable misfortune which retarded
progress and drove humanity off its course.[65]

In opposition to the completely determinate world of
the positivists Blanqui presents a picture of accident within
law which is quite similar to Engels' treatment of the problem.   Human volition can be the cause of change in a universe of law.   "A tiny incident can change the history of

61 *Ibid.*, 9592 (part 1), pp. 276-77.
62 *Ibid.*, p. 155.   63 *Ibid.*, 9590 (part 1), p. 181.
64 *Ibid.*, p. 187.   65 *Ibid.*, 9592 (part 1), p. 243.

humanity, without troubling in any way the invariable order which governs the world." [66]   Truly "no matter what
choice one makes one cannot escape fatality," but this is a
purely a posteriori fatality.   At every moment man is offered many alternatives.   In choosing one he abandons the
others forever—that is, commits himself to a particular consequence—but each specific choice is the product of the individual will.[67]

Thus it is the will of the individual which can exorcise
the bogey of political quietism raised by positivist theories
and by the consequences of a purely mechanistic materialism.   Blanqui, the avowed materialist, seems to call upon
Hegel for a characterization of man as both the agent and
product of endless change.   Man is subject to the "law of
opposites " and hence "the product of a slow but continuous transformation, a being who is always change, and
whose becoming is progress." [68]

[66] *Ibid.*, 9592 (part 1), p. 242.   Cf. Engels, *Ludwig Feuerbach*, p. 54:
"in human history, these laws assert themselves unconsciously in the
form of external necessity in the midst of an endless series of seeming
accidents."

[67] Blanqui, *L'Éternité par les astres*, p. 56.

[68] Blanqui MSS, 9590 (part 1), p. 187.

CHAPTER THREE

An Idealist Interpretation of Change and Its Consequences

THE ASSUMPTION that the human brain is the elemental agent of social progress has consequences for every aspect of Blanqui's social theory. We have seen that it enabled him to formulate a voluntarist political ideal within a determined universe on the assumption that progress could be attained through the biological transmission of cerebral improvements engendered by "the exercise of the brain by education." [1] Man was indeed a "sociable and perfectible animal," [2] and the source of his progress lay in the communication of thought.

The rejection of a strictly mechanistic explanation of individual development was reflected in Blanqui's theory of social change. Although a militant exponent of philosophic materialism, he actually thought of the Idea as the fundamental cause of political, social, and economic transformations. This attitude is implied in scattered statements to the effect that philosophy governs the world,[3] that the social milieu depends upon cerebral transformations,[4] and that revolutions must be made in the mind before they are made in the streets.[5] A more explicit formulation is Blanqui's list of forces that dominate society *"in the order of their power,"* as "Ideas, Capital, and Arms." [6]

[1] Blanqui MSS, 9592 (part 1), p. 155.
[2] *Ibid.*, p. 489.
[3] *Ibid.*, 9591 (part 1), p. 388.
[4] *Ni Dieu Ni Maître*, Nov. 30, 1880.
[5] Blanqui MSS, 9581, p. 149.   [6] *Ibid.*, 9591 (part 1), pp. 374-75.

An entry in Blanqui's notes, dated 1868, would seem to record his essential position on the relationship between the ideal and material aspects of social development. A recognition of the practical implications of the following paragraph is crucial to an understanding of Blanquism:

Poverty has only one cause, ignorance, the first cause which engenders all of the secondary causes. The material causes of poverty such as capitalism and all the other forms of exploitation only exist because of the ignorance of the masses.[7]

This statement is precisely the reverse of Marx's dictum that the nature of institutions is not to be grasped "from so-called progress of the human mind, but is rooted in the material conditions of life," which follows from his famous postulate, "It is not the consciousness of men that determines their being, but, on the contrary, their social existence that determines their consciousness." [8]

Here lies the fundamental and decisive philosophic separation of Marxism and Blanquism: significantly different interpretations of historical development, the nature of social revolution, and the tactics of a revolutionary party will arise out of this distinction.

The assumption that material and social relationships are determined by the degree of popular enlightenment is implied in a combined definition of philosophy and history: "To philosophize," wrote Blanqui, "is to study thought and knowledge; to write history is to give an account of the role of knowledge and thought in the life of humanity." [9]   Blanqui's brief analysis of the failure of the German peasant revolution in the sixteenth century is an

[7] *Ibid.*, 9592 (part 3), p. 159.

[8] K. Marx, *A Contribution to the Critique of Political Economy*, Tr. N. I. Stone (New York: The International Library Publishing Co., 1904), pp. 11-12.

[9] Blanqui MSS, 9590 (part 2), p. 488.

example of the application of this outlook to a specific historical situation. He observed that there could have been no successful revolution, nor any advance in liberty, at that period "without enlightenment," and he flatly concluded that the defeat of the peasants was "caused solely by ignorance." [10]

CLASSICISM, COMMUNISM, AND ENLIGHTENMENT

The above is an interpretation of history which recalls Condorcet's summation of the eighteenth-century view of human progress as the steady increase and dissemination of knowledge. Indeed, Blanqui's ideas of the past are permeated with the flavor of the era of the *philosophes*. He rejected the new historicism—the Gothic revival, the rediscovery of medieval culture, and the soothing genius of Christianity. He held to that veneration for classical antiquity and scorn for the Middle Ages which were the hallmark of neoclassicism.

In the culture of the ancient Greeks and Romans, Blanqui located the beginnings of materialism, science, and liberty. In fact, he asserted that the main components of what we call modern society were born of Greek and Roman genius.[11] This great flowering of the human spirit was destroyed by Christianity. The Church fathers ushered in a reign of terror, barbarism, and force which dominated Europe for twelve dark centuries, from the triumph of the "dogma of death" in the fourth century until the revolutionary invention of printing in the fifteenth.[12] Blanqui

[10] *Ibid.*, 9580, p. 29.

[11] *Ibid.*, 9592 (part 3), p. 355.

[12] *Ibid.*, 9590 (part 1), p. 157. Cf. Condorcet, *Esquisse d'un tableau historique des progrès de l'esprit humain* (Paris: Masson et Fils, 1822), p. 108: "The triumph of Christianity was thus the signal of the entire decline both of the sciences and of philosophy."

disapprovingly noted that many naïve democrats, disgusted with the vulgar commercial materialism of the crass age of Louis Philippe, longed for the supposed spirituality of Catholicism and manufactured a cult of the Middle Ages. This unfortunate aberration should long since have been effaced by the irrefutable evidence that Christianity is, and always has been, the mortal enemy of human progress.[13]

The thread of civilization had actually been severed by the Christian Middle Ages, only to be resumed at the reintroduction of classical studies in the sixteenth century.[14] Ever since that time the clergy has endeavored to thrust man back into the "night" of the fifteenth century, using every possible method including the "poisonous attempt" to curtail the study of Latin in the universities.[15] How gullible are the positivists to echo the canard that the Renaissance revival of classical learning was a retrogression, when, in reality, the ideas of "liberty and the Republic" had been preserved in the Greek and Latin tongues.[16]

Blanqui, the professional revolutionary, whose career is often described as the *nec plus ultra* of political romanticism,[17] in fact consciously and explicitly identified himself with the classical tradition. According to Geffroy, Blanqui's earliest intellectual influences were the classics, the histories of the Roman Republic, the French classical drama, and the Carbonarist movement with its "legions" and "cohorts" and its devotion to antique Republican purity.[18] Geffroy wrote that Blanqui supported the criticisms

[13] Blanqui MSS, 9590 (part 1), pp. 61-62 (dated 1869).

[14] *Ibid.*, 9587, p. 378.

[15] *Ibid.*, p. 336.

[16] *Ibid.*, 9590 (part 1), p. 65.

[17] R. Picard, *Le Romantisme social* (New York: Brentano's, 1944), p. 412.

[18] Geffroy, *L'Enfermé*, I, 38.

which Armand Carrel directed against Victor Hugo in the
name of literary classicism. He also relates an anecdote of
Blanqui's appearance, at the height of the July Revolution,
in Mlle de Montgolfier's salon. Blackened with powder
and blood, the young militant crashed his rifle butt against
the floor and cried triumphantly: "The Romantics are
done for!" These incidents, wrote Geffroy, showed Blanqui's "taste for order and harmony, his aversion to lyricism
and to Gothic phrases." [19]

There is actually no paradox in the union of Blanqui's
neoclassicism with his stormy and dramatic career. Out of
a strong faith in human reason, a desire for rational order
and harmony in everything, and the idealization of classic
models of civil rectitude, can develop the determination to
set the crazy world aright by translating logic into action
at any personal or social cost.

Ideas and values which Blanqui inherited from an ear-
lier milieu did undergo considerable transformation in the
face of changed circumstances and new ideas. Thus Blanqui, looking back from the nineteenth century, found
much to criticize in the naïve ideas of his spiritual fore-
bears. He scornfully described the St. Justs of the Revolutionary era as "fugitives from college," who, carried away
by classical rhetoric, fancied themselves the Ciceros and
Catilines of the Great Revolution, and paraded an ignorance of all "social questions" (i.e., economic problems)
that completely distorted their understanding of the past.[20]

Misrepresentations of history were to be corrected from
the socialist viewpoint. Revolutionaries must never model

[19] *Ibid.*, I, 53.
[20] Blanqui MSS, 9581, pp. 87-88. See H. T. Parker, *The Cult of
Antiquity and the French Revolutionaries* (Chicago: The University of
Chicago Press, 1937), *passim.*

themselves upon the rhetoricians of the Roman Republic, the Catos and Brutuses, who were the worst oligarchs and plunderers of the epoch. The true revolutionary is the heir neither of the patricians nor of the plebeians, but of their "common enemy, the people of the catacombs." [21] Essentially, Blanqui's criticism of an overindulgence in the classic pose was directed against the incorrect choice of antique models. He implicitly assumed the fundamental identity of man in any era but rejected an interpretation of the past which might obscure the contemporary distinction between socialist revolutionaries and bourgeois democrats.

To what one might call the neoclassical or rationalist interpretation of history as the progress of knowledge, Blanqui added notions borrowed from contemporary thinkers. The most important of these was the St. Simonian idea of "association," which was a key word in the new socio-economic vocabulary of the Utopian Socialists.[22] This word had been taken from St. Simon by his followers and given a socialistic connotation. According to the disciples of the great Utopian "the successive development of humanity recognizes only one law, and this law is the uninterrupted progress of association." [23]

Blanqui took the theory of increasing association as proof that social progress, although not fatally determined in the positivist sense, had been historically evident in the irregular but constant development of humanity from a

[21] *Ibid.*, pp. 233-34 (dated 1855).

[22] Tchernoff conjectures: "The Saint Simonian doctrine learned in the Society of the Friends of the People probably gave to Blanqui's ideas their definitive orientation on social questions." Tchernoff, *Le Parti républicain sous la Monarchie de Juillet*, p. 349.

[23] Quoted from *Doctrine Saint Simonienne—Exposition* (Paris: Librarie Nouvelle, 1854), p. 100. This is a collection of lectures given by the St. Simonians in 1829.

lower to a higher stage of social organization.[24] A description of this development is merely the story of "increasing association," which, for Blanqui, connoted any kind of social organization as opposed to individualism or anarchy, as well as the general spirit of human solidarity, or any specific acts of interpersonal cooperation.

The origins of association lay in the earliest examples of human cooperation. The individual was anterior to society and was moved by an instinct to develop at the expense of his fellows.[25] His desires were frustrated by the similar antisocial instincts of other men, and under these conditions, concluded Blanqui, mankind functioned as a species of intelligent beast. Until the individual began to realize that he was "nothing without society," [26] and began to act with others for common ends, he remained something less than "man."

After its first gigantic strides toward collective action, mankind progressed only through the extension of this "solidarity." In fact, "solidarity" became the agency of human selection in the Darwinian sense. This was the antithesis of the Social Darwinism which saw natural selection in the destruction of the weak, a theory which Blanqui castigated as scientifically invalid as well as socially pernicious. According to him, human selection "rests on association" and has functioned only through these feelings of solidarity which encourage the protection of the weak and thus set a limit to humanity's greatest danger—its self-destruction.[27]

---

[24] Blanqui MSS, 9590 (part 1), p. 182. Also L. A. Blanqui, *Critique sociale* (Paris: Félix Alcan, 1885), I, 173.

[25] Blanqui MSS, 9590 (part 1), pp. 177-80.

[26] *Ni Dieu Ni Maître,* Dec. 11, 1880.

[27] Blanqui MSS, 9590 (part 1), pp. 264-67 (probably written 1868).

Since progress could be defined in terms of the successive weakening of individualism or "increase in association," Blanqui concluded that its highest stage was to be communism.[28]   Therefore every progressive step—that is, every increment of social integration—is actually a communist innovation.   This implies the rejection of the familiar socialist hypothesis that primitive man dwelt in a collectivist paradise which subsequent developments had destroyed. Blanqui flatly asserted that communism could not have been "the confused syncretism of the earliest ages of humanity" but was to be "the last word of social science, the ideal of the future." [29]

In order to remove this postulate from the realm of the a priori, he attempted to refute the characterization of preagricultural society as communistic.   The most primitive peoples were not collectivists.   They individually held no property whatsoever, besides their hunting implements, so could scarcely have held property in common.   Nor could pastoral peoples who neither owned nor cultivated the land over which they roamed be described as communists.[30] Blanqui ignored the question as to whether tribal flocks did not constitute property held in common, and he implied a rather narrow definition of communism as the collective exploitation of landed property which has scarcity value.

Probably as early as 1834 he had already rejected any characterization of communism in the sense of a division and redistribution of land rather than its collective ownership.[31]   Nevertheless, he felt that the earliest division and

28 *Ni Dieu Ni Maître*, Dec. 10, 1880.
29 Blanqui, *Critique sociale*, II, 68.
30 *Ibid.*, pp. 68-78.
31 *Ibid.*, p. 126.

private appropriation of land was actually a step toward communism because of the necessary increase in social organization which it entailed. Every subsequent advance of "association" for the benefit of the exploiting minority was a step in the direction of a society which would mark the end of exploitation. The state, the postal service, the army, and the large industrial enterprise are all "communist innovations" which will some day deliver social justice out of the womb of a capitalist society. Capitalism would be destroyed by its own perfected instrument—the principle of association.[32]

Blanqui's triumphant faith in a communist millenium was qualified by his firm belief that any set of institutions directly depends upon the quality of the mass mind. He therefore cautioned that communism could never be established without full enlightenment. Truly, all efforts must be directed toward the welfare of the "collectivity" (i.e., society as a whole), "but the individual is the element of humanity," and with ignorant individuals nothing can be done.[33] Thus the social struggle must be consecrated to the enlightenment of the masses, and, at the same time, to the liberation of the individual mind from its institutional chains.

In practice all Utopian schemes, governmental reforms, and social improvements were useless without education [34] —the agent of progress, and "the force that governs the world." [35] The poor and downtrodden are oppressed pre-

32 *Ibid.*, I, 174-77.

33 Blanqui MSS, 9591 (part 2), p. 520.

34 *Ibid.*, 9592 (part 1), p. 500. Paul Lafargue recalled showing Blanqui a manuscript on socialist theory and being told: "All of these discussions on the forms of the future society are revolutionary scholasticism—it is more urgent to evaluate primary education." *La Révolution française,* April 20, 1879.

35 Blanqui MSS, 9581, p. 93.

cisely because of their ignorance and are often led to contribute to their own afflictions. "Ignorance is at the same
time the instrument and the victim of violence." [36] Enlightenment was the precondition, on the one hand, for a
successful social revolution and, on the other, for the good
society that the revolution was to create. Education was
"the only real revolutionary agent"; [37] it was *Liberté
Égalité, Fraternité*,[38] and the chances for a basic social upheaval were slim indeed as long as the mind of the masses
remained in thrall.[39]

Even if a revolution were successfully consummated in
an unenlightened society no permanently satisfactory social
organization could result. Communism, the highest social
form, could never be politically improvised because it was
a consequence of enlightenment rather than its cause.[40]
No matter what formal economic or political institutions
humanity establishes, it can never truly emancipate itself
until, "thanks to universal enlightenment, not one man
can be the dupe of another." [41]

At his most optimistic, Blanqui drew the corollary that
communism would, in fact, be the infallible result of universal secular compulsory education. Some of his writings
leave the impression of a naïve faith in the wonderful results of sending everyone to public school. He even asserted that a *lycée* education for everyone would guarantee
the reign of absolute equality,[42] and that if freedom of
speech and the press were added to universal public education, within ten years *all* exploitation would have ceased.[43]

---

36 Blanqui, *Critique sociale*, I, 212.
37 Blanqui MSS, 9581, p. 23 (dated 1848).
38 *Ibid.*, 9580, p. 29.
39 Blanqui, *Critique sociale*, I, 96.
40 *Ibid.*, p. 186.   41 *Ibid.*, p. 185.
42 *Ibid.*, pp. 211-12.   43 *Ibid.*, II, 160.

This is the environmentalism of a happier age, a reaffirmation of Condorcet's assurance that "the progress of virtue has ever accompanied that of knowledge." [44]   However, this fragile last flowering of the eighteenth century could not maintain itself against the icy realities of Blanqui's own era. In 1870, when the products of Prussia's famous educational system trampled across Blanqui's beloved France, he flatly repudiated the theory that universal education necessarily guarantees a high level of national intelligence. The unthinking and reactionary Teuton hordes had been raised on stupid and reactionary ideas, and thus were brutalized, rather than improved, by their education: "a student nourished on nonsense becomes a fool." [45]

Even before the Franco-Prussian war, Blanqui had recognized the fact that literacy in itself was only a means and that intellectual progress depended upon what was read as well as what proportion of the population was literate.[46] The values of those who control the organs of public enlightenment would determine the quality of the public mind, and this is the reason that one could reconcile the advocacy of a political revolution with the belief that progress is impossible without education. A complete dependence upon the peaceful spread of knowledge as the motor of progress guaranteed in practice the untroubled ability of the ruling classes to suppress or distort those ideas which carried the germ of their destruction.

Blanqui was aware of the possible gradualist implications of his views on the necessity of enlightenment and several times attempted to forestall them. He feared that

[44] Condorcet, *Esquisse d'un tableau historique des progrès de l'esprit humain*, pp. 79-80.
[45] *Le Châtiment*, March 3, 1871, "Un Dernier mot par A. Blanqui."
[46] Blanqui MSS, 9592 (part 1), p. 142 (dated 1868).

his admission that ignorance was the precondition of exploitation might be used as an argument for the adjournment of the "social question" until after the complete education of the masses. In estimating the relative perniciousness of ignorance, on the one hand, and "vampirism" of the capitalist, on the other, he wrote:

of these two harpies which is the mother? Which is the daughter? Study of the past and observation seem to prove that ignorance is the mother. A dangerous conclusion, nevertheless, which will furnish pretexts for the adjournment of social questions, pretexts which have long been used in order to postpone indefinitely the emancipation of the Negroes. The attack ought to be opened and carried out simultaneously against these two bastions of iniquity.[47]

RELIGION—THE IDEA OF OPPRESSION

The combination of Blanqui's idealist philosophy of social development, his interpretation of the past as a struggle between classical enlightenment and medieval obscurantism, and his belief that political activity should be directed against institutions which inhibited mental development was the logical basis for his preoccupation with the fundamental and pernicious role of religion and the Church in the social order. His political milieu was traditionally anticlerical, and the Catholic Church was, in nineteenth-century France, one of the most consistent and powerful political enemies of all the republican and socialist values to which Blanqui had committed his life. Whatever the genesis of Blanqui's anticlericalism, it was for him not merely a standard item in the French radical's intellectual equipment, or a traditional leftist political tactic, but one of the foundations of his entire social and political philosophy.

[47] Blanqui, *Critique sociale,* II, 41 (dated 1867).

Committed to a belief in the fundamental social role of ideas, and the revolutionary political role of public education, Blanqui saw the Church as the most powerful institution perpetuating human ignorance and political oppression. In the modern world Christianity survived not as an unfortunate consequence of unjust social relationships, but as one of their most fundamental causes, and perhaps as their most effective preserver.[48]

Blanqui began his political career with that hostility to the Catholic Church which was the patrimony of the Great Revolution, but in his early years he retained some belief in an essentially benevolent Supreme Being.[49] Eventually he relinquished even the mildest deism for a brand of aggressive atheism which found evil incarnate in the very work "God." This evil concept had become an essential element in all techniques of human exploitation; it was the monstrous idea which placed force at the service of intelligence in order to exterminate humanity.[50]

All religious values had proved themselves to be part of the paraphernalia of oppression, and all sects had devoted themselves to its practice. The Jews, the Protestants, and the Mohammedans have, equally with the Catholics, inhumanity in their hearts and blood on their hands. According to Blanqui, the so-called Protestant Reformation had only the unfortunate effect of shoring up the tottering structure of European Christianity while the "reformers" committed new crimes beneath the banners of such "monstrous fanatics" as Luther and Calvin. Of the two great Christian sects, Catholicism has been the "tomb of intelli-

48 Blanqui MSS, 9590 (part 2), p. 356.
49 *Les Lettres*, Sept. 6, 1908 (in a letter from Blanqui dated Feb. 12, 1834).
50 *Ni Dieu Ni Maître*, Nov. 21, 1880.

gence, thought, and the brain; Protestantism, the grave of the conscience, sentiment, and the heart." [51]   Characteristically, Blanqui assigned the greater guilt to the Catholic Church because the destruction of intelligence would truly mean the end of all human progress.[52]

He reserved most of his anticlerical ammunition for Christianity in general and the Catholic Church in particular. Christianity has been the most ferocious of these "terrible monotheistic sects" which have outdone the worst crimes of the so-called primitive religions.[53] Christianity has become the first cause of contemporary social injustice because it has turned the people into a herd of docile beasts to be led into the hands of the capitalists and aristocrats.[54] Thus the modern world has witnessed "a permanent conspiracy of capital and clericalism" and is crushed under the combined weight of the "sacristy, stock exchange, and military barracks." [55]

Unfortunately the average worker, not recognizing the source of his misfortune, does not sufficiently hate and fear the Church. This social myopia has been fostered by his poor education, which is the product of a conspiracy between the government and the Church.[56] The workers are exploited to pay for those clerical schools which are the best support and last hope of capitalism.[57]

In Blanqui's eyes, the manipulation of the educational system in order to inhibit the enlightenment of the masses was the supreme social crime. As late as 1850, he was still

[51] Blanqui MSS, 9581, p. 52.
[52] *Ibid.,* p. 372.
[53] *Ibid.,* 9587, p. 303.
[54] *Ibid.,* 9571 (part 1), p. 376.
[55] Quoted in M. Dommanget, "L'Athéisme et l'anti-catholicisme de Blanqui," *Bulletin Rationaliste,* July, 1952, p. 4.
[56] Blanqui MSS, 9591 (part 1), pp. 375-76.
[57] Blanqui, *Critique sociale,* II, 354 (dated 1869).

able to regard the struggle over clerical schools in France from the standpoint of a socialist hostility towards both combatants. At that time he felt that two reactionary groups were struggling for the control of France, and one, "the Voltairian *bourgeoisie*," would be unable to consolidate its rule as long as the "Jesuits" controlled educational facilities.[58]

He relinquished this indifference during the course of the Second Empire as the clerical schools flourished in competition with the secular Université.[59] He began to follow the controversy over "free" as opposed to secular education with increasing interest and partisanship. He eventually concluded that since Christianity was the bulwark of the most reactionary elements in French society, anyone who did not wholeheartedly defend secular education against the encroachments of the Jesuits was on the side of clerical reaction, no matter what his pretended political affiliation.[60]

The intellectualized religion affected by many social reformers was to Blanqui a subtle form of intellectual chicanery, ultimately as pernicious as outright clericalism. The new social religions manufactured by St. Simon, Fourier, and Comte [61] would end as mere historical curiosities along with the exhortations of that "strange and amphibious breed of intellectual hermaphrodites, the Christian Socialists, whose very name was a contradiction in terms." [62] Also to be reproached were all those "liberals"

---

[58] Blanqui MSS, 9581, p. 299.

[59] C. Seignobos, *La Révolution de 1848—Le Second Empire*, Vol. VI of *Histoire de France contemporaine*, ed. E. Lavisse (Paris: Libraire Hachette, 1921), p. 150.

[60] Blanqui, *Critique sociale*, I, 180.

[61] Blanqui MSS, 9592 (part 1), p. 492.

[62] *Ibid.*, 9583, p. 99.

who confused the people with equivocal phrases, such as the assertion that they were "more truly religious than the priests," which essentially supported clericalism.[63]   Christianity had been slain "by the hand of Voltaire" and all attempts to revive it in the nineteenth century were only the exhumation of a corpse.[64]

Blanqui predicted that "the nineteenth century will only justify itself through Science." [65]   Therefore, the refusal of many scientists to accept the atheist consequences of their investigations was especially reprehensible.   Science, in in spite of itself, was destroying the foundations of religion, and only cowardice or intellectual treason kept the scientist from boldly dissipating the phantoms of religiosity forever.[66]

Blanqui observed with disgust the beginnings of the attempts, so familiar in the twentieth century, to justify religion by appeals to science.   The abbé Gratry, a popular liberal theologian and member of the Academy, had published a brochure which argued the scientific basis of religious dogma.   Blanqui devoted a series of very characteristic articles in the short-lived radical and atheist journal, *Candide,* to a sarcastic attack on the religio-science of Gratry.[67]

As far as the old atheist was concerned, Gratry's modern Catholic synthesis was merely the clerical retirement before the forces of truth to new prepared positions.   The Reverend Father, he observed, had, for example, been enchanted

[63] *Ibid.,* 9590 (part 1), p. 170.

[64] *Ibid.,* p. 62.

[65] *Ibid.*

[66] *Ibid.,* 9591 (part 1), pp. 389-90.

[67] The articles were collected in a pamphlet: *Foi et Science ou la Science du R. P. Gratry par "Suzamel"* (Bruxelles: Typographie de D. Bresmee, 1866).   See especially pp. 5-15.

by the discovery of astronomical principles which enabled him scientifically to explain the scriptural prediction that "the stars will fall from heaven." Beware, warned Blanqui, of attempting to explain the miraculous by anything but miracles. What scientific principles will explain Joshua's miracle of the temporary cessation of terrestial rotation? Will Gratry dare to reject the smallest Biblical residue of unscientific dogma? It is far better to rest in the Catholic tradition, and threaten "reason with anathema," than to lose one's way in the halls of science.

The attack upon Gratry is one example of the countless fragmentary notes, paragraphs, and short articles which Blanqui directed against religion and the Catholic Church. Probably the majority of his salvaged manuscript writings are committed to what he considered the great revolutionary task of anticlerical polemic. Not only did he combat the philosophic justification of religion, he was ready to attack it on any level, from sarcastic rationalist caricatures of the catechism to caustic reflections on the possible prurience of St. Jerome.[68]

In the tradition of French anticlericalism, Blanqui devoted extended polemics to the history of religious intolerance. The murder of a Hellenic intellectual by a Christian mob in the fourth century,[69] Biblical accounts of the slaughter of pagans by the Jews,[70] and the murderous destruction of the Anabaptist community at Munster[71] are examples used as ammunition for his ceaseless bombardment of the religious edifice.

Blanqui angrily defended atheists against imputations that they were the advocates of "sordid materialism."

[68] Blanqui MSS, 9590 (part 1), pp. 510-12.
[69] Ibid., pp. 495-501.   [70] Ibid., 9587, p. 381.
[71] Ibid., 9581, p. 171.

They had been accused of the worst criminal potentialities, and then brutally harassed and murdered by the generations of the faithful. True spirituality remained with the materialists who did not need to base their morality upon a debased fetishism and a brutal system of punishments which had led to the intellectual degeneration of entire peoples.[72] The Breton peasant always served Blanqui as a typical product of clerical brutalization—his precise antithesis was, of course, the enlightened atheistic Paris worker.[73] The afflictions of a society dominated by the Church were even more acute in other Latin countries— witness the debased and impoverished peoples of Italy, Spain, and South America. In those countries, Blanqui sardonically wrote, one can estimate the number of prostitutes a nation supports by counting the Madonnas it displays.[74]

Not only was organized religion the fountainhead of social degeneracy, it was absolute death to any revolutionary movement which came under its influence. Movements for national liberation in countries such as Poland and Ireland were doomed to failure as long as they retained their connection with clerical-feudal elements who led them only to betray them.[75] For many years Blanqui was also hostile to the Risorgimento, not only because of Mazzini's antisocialism, but because of the religiosity of the movement.[76] Blanqui argued that any revolution worthy of the name or carrying any hope of permanent success must begin by sweeping away religion, root and branch.[77] The supreme

[72] *Ni Dieu Ni Maître,* Dec. 11, 1880.
[73] *Ibid.*
[74] *Ibid.,* Dec. 12, 1880.
[75] Blanqui MSS, 9487, p. 336.
[76] *Ibid.,* 9584 (part 1), p. 65.
[77] *Ibid.,* 9590 (part 2), p. 325.

error of the Great Revolution had in fact been its failure to fulfill the very reason for its existence, *la destruction prélate du Christianisme dans l'esprit de ses auteurs.*[78]

In Blanqui's eyes, Robespierre was the arch traitor to the revolution, primarily because he had rejected atheism and taken his place among the "bloody champions of God."[79] Robespierre killed the Revolution in three blows: the execution of Hébert, that of Danton, and the establishment of an altar to the Supreme Being.[80] With his cult of the Supreme Being, Robespierre had revived the slaughtered monster of religion, and thus confused and shattered the *élan* of "the people" who from that time forth had washed their hands of a revolution which had betrayed their professed desires.[81]

The practical significance of an idealist theory of social development is clearly seen when one contrasts Blanqui's ideas on the political role of anticlericalism with those of Lenin. The Russian leader did, indeed, advocate a constant effort against "all religious deception of the workers," a persistent atheist propaganda, which in capitalist countries would take the form of the struggle to separate Church and State, but he categorically rejected "Blanquist or anarchist insistence" that the war on religion was a political objective of a workers' party. Since the basis of religion was primarily social, the attempt to unify the proletariat in its fight against capitalism should never be jeopardized by alienating those workers who had as yet been unable to free themselves from the intellectual concomitants of fundamental social relationships. "The unity of that genuinely revolutionary struggle of the oppressed class

[78] *Ibid.*, 9592 (part 3), p. 412.
[79] *Ibid.*, 9581, pp. 77-78.
[80] *Ibid.*, 9581, p. 83.   [81] *Ibid.*, pp. 83-84.

to set up a heaven on earth is more important to us than a unity in proletarian opinion about the imaginary paradise in the sky." [82]

On the other hand Blanqui, who believed that "the social milieu depends upon cerebral transformations," [83] saw proletarian enlightenment as the absolute precondition of a successful revolution. The "social" and religious questions were, therefore, identical. An abandonment of the fight to destroy religion was a surrender to it, and consequently a renunciation of the dream of revolution. Blanqui's reluctance to outline plans for the day after the revolution never inhibited his promising to take the first step into the postrevolutionary world over the corpse of Christianity. Drastic surgery was indicated for a world "sick from Christianity" for twelve hundred years.[84] This revolutionary necessity was all the more categorical in a period which had witnessed the coalescence of all reactionary forces under the pressure of increasing popular resistance to tyranny. There were now only two parties to the political conflict: "Jesuits and Socialists." [85]

[82] V. I. Lenin, *Religion,* Vol. VII of *Little Lenin Library* (New York: International Publishers, 1933), pp. 7-10.

[83] *Ni Dieu Ni Maître,* Nov. 30, 1880.

[84] Blanqui MSS, 9592 (part 3), p. 412.

[85] *Ibid.,* 9581, p. 303. It is interesting to recall the words of Dostoyevsky in this connection: "For socialism is not merely the labor question, it is before all things the atheistic question, the question of the form taken by atheism today, the question of the tower of Babel built without God, not to mount to Heaven from earth but to set up Heaven on earth." F. Dostoyevsky, *The Brothers Karamazov,* tr. C. Garnett (New York: Random House, 1933), p. 23.

CHAPTER FOUR

Economic Theory

BLANQUI'S BATTLE CRY, "War on the supernatural, that is the enemy," [1] sounded the note of a political tradition which extends from Voltaire to Gambetta—from *écrasez l'infâme* to *Le cléricalisme, voilà l'ennemi*. He departed from this tradition, and the slogans of the French liberal *bourgeoisie*, when he declared that the "palm of evil" might as well be awarded to usurious capitalism as to the idea of God.[2] The capitalists, the aristocrats, and the clergy were allies whom the revolution must impartially destroy.

In applying the ideals of the Great Revolution to the economic injustices of nineteenth-century society, Blanqui joined the ranks of those who set out on the paradoxical voyage from the Declaration of the Rights of Man to the dictatorship of the proletariat—that is, from the literal acceptance of libertarian political values to the conviction that they might only be realized through the forcible transformation of economic institutions.

In Blanqui's evaluation of the revolutionary trinity of Liberty, Equality, and Fraternity, the outlines of one road from Jacobinism to socialism can be clearly discerned. On this road the signpost is "Equality"—for Blanqui, "the sublime revelation" [3] which was the absolute condition for the

---

1 Blanqui MSS, 9590 (part 2), p. 486.

2 Blanqui, *Critique sociale*, I, 43.

3 Quoted from a handwritten copy of Blanqui's newspaper *Le Libérateur* (1834), in Blanqui's MSS, 9592 (part 3), pp. 4-5.

existence of Liberty and Fraternity. In fact Liberty was
but a chimera if not based upon Equality. Furthermore,
the very word Liberty had been so misused and dishonored
by disguised reactionaries that true revolutionaries might
just as well temporarily dispense with it.[4] Fraternity, too,
was absolutely conditioned by Equality, for Fraternity
meant nothing more than "the impossibility of killing
one's brother," and therefore could only exist among equals.
"Security for each individual exists only in universal equality of power." [5] Blanqui qualified his rationalist faith in
the liberating force of enlightenment to admit that, without equality of power, even education was no guarantee of
Liberty and Fraternity.[6]

The professional revolutionary was characteristically
vague on the precise social nature of the equality he invoked, but vigorous and definite as to the inequalities to
which he was opposed. In his early writings he referred in
a very general way to the "life and death struggle . . . between privilege and equality," and identified himself with
all of the oppressed, "whether exploited by the sword or by
gold." [7] In the early '30s he still thought in terms of a
broad moral and political struggle in which Jesus Christ,
Gregory VII, and Robespierre were all paladins of justice,[8]
but he was already beginning to lend to the word Equality
economic connotations which were to carry him far from
the vague humanitarianism of his youth.

In 1834 he predicted the inevitable disappearance of human slavery, which would be the first blow struck by the
"principle of equality" against the "sacred right of property." This would inevitably be followed by the extirpa-

---

[4] Blanqui MSS, 9590 (part 1), p. 170.
[5] *Ibid.*, pp. 179-80.   [6] *Ibid.*, p. 180.
[7] From the copy of *Le Libérateur* (1834), cited, p. 5.
[8] *Ibid.*

tion of that modern slave system which existed so long as most men were deprived of the "instruments of their labor" for the benefit of a possessing minority. "It is this monopoly, and not some political constitution or other which enslaves the masses." [9]

It is actually not surprising to discover that Blanqui, the conspirator and activist, wrote in these terms. In the nineteenth century, egalitarian social and political values were increasingly phrased in terms of economic relationships. Time and again in writings and speeches between 1834 and 1880, Blanqui committed himself and his party to the attainment of equality through socialism. The economic theory with which he buttressed his anticapitalist polemics contained little analysis of a socialist future, but a great deal of criticism of the contemporary economic system. Blanqui's "socialist" economic theory is embodied in his declaration: "The very essence of socialism lies in this formula: Illegitimacy of the interest on capital." [10] It is upon the ancient condemnation of usury that Blanqui bases his revolutionary anticapitalism.

THE ATTACK ON USURY

Blanqui's notes on economics occupy the largest amount of space in his published writings. They are a blend of weak a priori hypotheses and vigorous critical insights into the malfunctionings of the contemporary economic system. For Blanqui, political economy was not a positive, but a

[9] Blanqui, *Critique sociale*, II, 120. From an article "Qui fait la soupe doit la manger," which was to appear in Blanqui's newspaper *Le Libérateur* in 1834. Only one issue of the paper was published, and this article was not included. During the 1850s Blanqui revised the piece, and it was eventually published in his *Critique sociale*. It is impossible to say how many ideas were changed or added in the revision.

[10] Blanqui, *Critique sociale*, II, 150.

normative, discipline. He warned the reader that he did not intend to present a professional economic treatise, but "a series of insights relating to social questions . . . the order of the arguments is of little importance as long as they hit the mark." [11]   An examination of these arguments forces one to agree that Blanqui did often sacrifice theory to polemic.

The historical scaffolding for Blanqui's economic theory was his idea of the development of the exchange mechanism from primitive barter to a money economy. He described the transition from a pastoral economy to an agrarian society based on the personal appropriation of land as a concomitant of the gradual change from an economy of self-sufficiency and barter to one of a rudimentary division of labor and a relatively complex system of exchange.[12] To Blanqui, the mechanism by which the equivalence between goods to be exchanged is maintained in a complex economy was the key to an understanding of economics. "The base of exchange is the equivalence of objects to be exchanged." [13]

Without offering any detailed evidence, Blanqui asserted that, in some pioneering epoch, the precious metals (and later the more convenient coins which were minted from them) were discovered to be the providential means for maintaining equivalence through a complex series of economic transactions. Unfortunately they were also the vehicle for the perversion of a system of equivalence by the introduction of "interest." Usury was not a necessary consequence of a money economy, but historically its inevitable accompaniment.[14] It was "usury"—that is, the taking

11 *Ibid.*, I, 1 (dated 1869).   12 *Ibid.*, II, 78-81.
13 *Ibid.*, I, 22.   14 *Ibid.*, I, 45.

of interest—which guaranteed the ultimate inequity and illegitimacy of any conceivable capitalist system.

With the creaking device of a dialogue between two
representative economic men, Blanqui attempted to demonstrate the capitalist misuse of money which must inevitably
destroy the "natural" system of equivalence.[15] The hero
of the dialogue is the worker "Lazare," who argues vigorously against usury with brilliant irony couched in literary
and classical allusions. These are usually lost on "Gobseck," the uncultured capitalist boor who offers only the
most obvious and moth-eaten arguments against the eru-
dite sarcasm of his proletarian antagonist.

Each of these economic personifications, the poor but
honest worker and the greedy money lender, is assumed to
have originally produced an amount of goods equal in
value to the production of the other. Both need to exchange the goods they cannot personally consume for an
equivalent amount of other necessities. This reciprocal exchange must be carried out through the medium of money,
which functions as the convenient measure of the equivalence existing between the products.

One of the men, the virtuous proletarian, spends all of
the money he received for his surplus product on other
goods, thus consuming the equivalent of his total production. The nascent usurer, on the other hand, denies himself and his family a part of the goods he ought to buy in
order to retain as a store of value some of the money he received for his surplus product. Then the man who has
dutifully consumed the full equivalent of his own product
is to be denied that portion of the market for his goods
which Gobseck's abstention has eliminated. Poor Lazare

15 *Ibid.*, pp. 12-38.

is left with an unsold surplus which no longer buys him its
equivalent in necessities.

In order to fill the gap in his larder, which can no
longer be replenished by selling his own goods, he must
borrow the cash equivalent of the unsold goods. Enter the
usurer, who now gathers the fruits of his underconsumption. His unused cash can be borrowed, but he demands a
payment for its use. When the loan has been repaid he
will have gained an increment beyond the amount he
should have received in a "legitimate" equivalent exchange. This unjust increment is the interest he charged
for the loan.

Blanqui then endeavored to show that the original good
consumer, indebted to the usurer, and absolutely unable to
close the increasing gap between his needs and his receipts,
hires himself out at a wage to his avaricious creditor. He
then receives a sum which is less than the value of the
goods he creates by precisely the amount of "interest"
which the entrepreneur is realizing on his capital investment. At this point Blanqui has obviously combined with
his crude underconsumption theory a variation of the familiar labor theory of value. In order to explain how capitalist expropriation through the taking of interest actually
occurs in a wage-labor economy, he more or less implicitly
assumes that all value is created by labor. "Wealth is the
product of intelligence and labor . . . capital goods are
sterile in themselves, they are only fructified by labor." [16]

However, it is not any exproporiation of a "surplus
value" which is the original capitalist sin, but the underconsumption which accumulates the capital in the first
place. When this capital is invested, the interest realized
upon it is a further usurpation of part of the value im-

16 *Ibid.*, II, 118-19.

parted to a product by the worker. The entrepreneur is indeed entitled to a profit insofar as it represents a just reward for his managerial abilities; he is justified in setting aside sums for raw materials and depreciation of fixed equipment; but the amount he withdraws as interest on his initial investment is money stolen from the worker's pocket.[17]

The category, "interest," from which all unjust expropriations flow, includes dividends, ground rents, house rents, discounts on commercial paper, charges for pawning, or any levy on the use of goods or the use of what we would call "capital." [18]   One might well ask: "What exactly is capital in Blanqui's economic cosmos?"   According to Blanqui, the definition of capital had been purposely obscured by the bourgeois political economists in order to mislead and confuse the simple and credulous. The professional economists have variously, and often simultaneously, defined capital as: the total accumulation of goods, all objects whose value has been improved by labor, and all goods which create value in other goods. Capital, insisted Blanqui, was none of these things, nor could it be described as "accumulated labor." It is not accumulated labor, but "suppressed and stolen labor." [19] More precisely, capital is only the accumulation of unspent cash; it is nothing but the stock of money which represents the total "interest" gained from the evil practices of "saving." In short, capital, interest, and savings are identical—a cash levy laid on the producing masses by the capitalist underconsumers.[20]

The postulates of Blanquist economics are hardly original. The idea of exchange as an expression of an original equivalence between quantities of goods has an ancient

17 *Ibid.*, I, 29-30.   18 *Ibid.*, p. 82.
19 *Ibid.*, p. 63.   20 *Ibid.*, pp. 53-72.

pedigree. From Aristotle to Marx, a series of theoreticians, including most of the great classical economists and the French political economists of the early nineteenth century, has reasoned from this assumption. It was not until the emergence of the subjective value theorists in the last third of the nineteenth century that the idea of equivalence was seriously questioned.[21]

Blanqui's theory of the "neutral" function of money—that it should act only as a convenient standard of equivalence and any profit on its use is immoral—was so close to Aristotle's observations on the subject that one might conjecture a direct influence. In Aristotle's *Nichomachean Ethics* is the assertion:

all things that are exchanged must be somehow comparable. . . . It is for this end that money has been introduced. . . . Money then acting as a measure, makes goods commensurate and weights them.[22]

And, from the *Politics:*

money was intended to be used in exchange, and not to increase at interest. . . . Wherefor of all modes of wealth, this is the most unnatural.[23]

Blanqui often referred to interest as "unnatural," or "illegitimate," or "illicit"—in fact his normative treatment of economic phenomena is reminiscent not only of the great classical thinkers, but of the medieval civilization which Blanqui so despised.[24] Sometimes his hatred of interest

[21] See K. Menger, *Principles of Economics,* tr. Dingwall and Hoselitz (Glencoe: The Free Press, 1950), p. 192; for a critique of the theory of equivalence, and p. 305 for a bibliographical sketch of some major proponents of the theory.

[22] Aristotle, "The Nichomachean Ethics," *Introduction to Aristotle,* ed. Richard McKeon (New York: The Modern Library, 1947), pp. 408-10.

[23] Aristotle, *Politics,* tr. B. Jowett (New York: The Modern Library, 1943), Book I. chap. 10, pp. 71-72.

[24] Cf. E. Whittaker, *A History of Economic Ideas* (New York: Longmans, Green and Co., 1940), pp. 516-23.

and the usurers seems to have more in common with the thirteenth century than with the nineteenth, although to this day the usurer is still the bogey of certain varieties of lower-middle-class or peasant radicalism.[25]

To his rather anachronistic analysis of the workings of the capitalist system Blanqui added an assortment of the ideas of French economic thinkers of the seventeenth and eighteenth centuries. His belief in the vital role of the precious metals in the functioning of a complex economy led him not only to decry the use of paper money and modern credit instruments,[26] but to accept the old mercantilist shibboleth of bullionism. This nineteenth-century socialist firmly believed that an outward flow of precious metals must inevitably lead to national impoverishment, and that their possession was the very foundation of national wealth.[27]

Blanqui also carried over into his century that idea of the physiocrats that the true riches of a nation lie in its agriculture and that commerce is an essentially parasitic occupation.[28] In words very similar to those of Holbach on the same subject,[29] he asserted that national power "founded on the factory and the counting house is ephemeral power," citing the brief splendor of nations such as Athens, Venice, and Holland as evidence of the inevitable fall of commercial peoples.[30]

The primary function of this rather disjointed theorizing was obviously polemical. Blanqui must have felt the need for some theoretical basis for his *ad hoc* critique of the inequities of the economic order, as well as for his rather

[25] See p. 80 below.
[26] Blanqui, *Critique sociale*, II, 28-33.
[27] *Ibid.*, I, 168-72.
[28] See G. Weulersse, *Les Physiocrates* (Paris: Gaston Doin et Cie., 1931), pp. 69-73.
[29] D'Holbach, *La Politique naturelle* (London: 1773), II, 156-57.
[30] Blanqui, *Critique sociale*, II, 12.

effective attacks upon the academic defenders of the economic *status quo*. Indeed, Blanqui's weak socialist economics was the reverse of the poor neoclassical coin which was circulated by the French economists as the genuine British article.

THE ATTACK ON POLITICAL ECONOMY

Many of Blanqui's articles were directed against contemporary French economists, especially Frederic Bastiat, the influential exponent of free trade and absolute free enterprise who popularized and unconsciously caricatured the great edifice of British political economy. Blanqui and Bastiat arrived at their antithetical conclusions from common assumptions of exchange and interest as the motors of capitalist enterprise, and from common techniques of reasoning by oversimplified analogy. For Bastiat, equivalence of exchange was admirably maintained in a money economy free from state interference; [31] for Blanqui, it was inevitably perverted by the introduction of interest. For both Bastiat and Blanqui, interest was a reward for accumulation, a vital spring of industrial progress to the former and an illicit unearned increment to the latter.

In characteristic fashion Blanqui framed his criticisms of orthodox political economy in terms of morality. The classical apotheosis of thrift and saving was, in Blanqui's eyes, a deliberate ruse to encourage the very process which destroyed the "natural" system of equivalence and begot all of the evils of usury. The most profligate wastrel or idle spendthrift was preferable to the thrifty bourgeois idea of the academicians.[32] The various definitions of "capital" which disguised the fact that it was the cash accumulation

[31] F. Bastiat, *Essays on Political Economy*, tr. David A. Wells (New York: G. P. Putnam and Sons, 1877), p. 18.
[32] Blanqui, *Critique sociale*, I, 78-79.

of the illicit gains of usury were fruits of conscious attempts to obscure its truly evil character by contradictory and confusing formulations.[33]

The pretentions of political economy to an amoral scientific objectivity enraged the dedicated revolutionary. The economists were prepared to sanction the worst injustices in the name of "law"—but this "law" was only a matter of fact description of an institutionalized code of "mutual extermination."[34] The academicians, among whom his brother Adolphe held an eminent position, were, for Blanqui, the paid lackeys and apologists of capitalism.

Like many of his socialist contemporaries, Blanqui was on firmer ground when he eschewed pure theory to catalogue the discrepancies between economic reality and its image in the works of the political economists. Although lacking their powers of systematic exposition, he was able upon occasion to attack their rather arid optimism with considerable effect.

Bastiat and his fellows imagined a world of almost perfect social and economic mobility, in which perseverance, thrift, and intelligence were always rewarded by commercial success and every worker carried the baton of a captain of industry in his knapsack. Blanqui dryly observed that in fact no army can support more than a handful of marshals, and that Bastiat offered nothing to the worker but the "hope" of becoming a capitalist in a society where the proportion of the self-employed was steadily decreasing.[35] Furthermore, the orthodox model of the supply-and-demand price mechanism was belied by the real situation. The so-called "value" or social wealth which capitalist

[33] *Ibid.*, pp. 131-33.   [34] *Ibid.*, p. 141.
[35] *Ibid.*, pp. 117-22.

entrepreneurs were supposed to produce in a free market was actually directed into their own pockets by price-raising techniques of monopolistic underproduction.[36]

Although the growth of monopoly in France did not compare with that of the great industrial nations,[37] Blanqui noted the tendencies of economic polarization by which the medium and small enterprises were swallowed up by the large:

On the ruins of small-scale enterprise has arisen the terrible financial, industrial, and commercial feudality which is cleverer and more oppressive than the old aristocracy, and holds our entire society in fee.[38]

The very techniques of superior organization with which high finance was changing the face of the economy would someday be the engine of its destruction, for this capitalist intensification of "association" must ultimately result in communism.[39] By combining the St. Simonian theory of "association" with his own observations of the economic system, Blanqui had briefly asserted the inevitable victory of his cause as inherent in the development of the existing order. This element, so crucial to the Marxian cosmos, was, of course, definitely subordinated to the voluntarist content of Blanqui's political ideas.

Blanqui also found the objective conditions for his apocalypse in the process of mass impoverishment which he, like so many others, felt to be concomitant with capitalist industrial expansion. All of the vaunted technological advances and increasing productivity of capitalism had but

[36] *Ibid.*, p. 175.

[37] J. H. Clapham, *The Economic Development of France and Germany, 1815-1914* (4th ed.; Cambridge: University Press, 1951), pp. 257-58.

[38] Blanque, *Critique sociale*, I, 176.

[39] *Ibid.*, pp. 176-77.

served to depress proletarian living standards. England, the glory of the capitalist century, was the home of the most shocking extremes of wealth and poverty.[40] The continuous expansion of productive capacity only increased the gap between production and the consumption of the masses, and thus there appeared those continued crises of unemployment and overproduction which no iteration of Say's law could disguise. For Blanqui this was the practical demonstration of his theory of underconsumption and interest. The consuming potential of the masses was reduced by the capitalist extortion of "interest" from the workers' product.[41] As the ability of the masses to consume decreased, a continuous domestic plethora led to the contest for world markets and to that ferocious European exploitation of backward nations which made "the white race a legitimate object of execration for four-fifths of humanity" [42]

The persistent juxtaposition of outworn economic concepts and rather prescient criticisms of contemporary capitalism becomes more explicable if referred to the economy which Blanqui attempted to analyze. By the middle of the century Blanqui was well into his forties and had, in all probability, worked out most of the postulates of his economic thinking. His ideas were developed in reference to an economy which, to this day, has never been completely conquered by industrial capitalism, during a period characterized by the limited but unsettling advance of modern industrialism into a predominantly agrarian society.

THE BACKGROUND OF THE THEORY

In 1850, France boasted important regions of industrial concentration but was still chiefly a land of peasant enter-

40 Ibid., II, 306-8.   41 Ibid., p. 30.
42 Ibid., p. 27 (dated 1870).

prise. Only 10 percent of the French population lived in towns of 20,000 or more inhabitants.[43] Of these scattered mercantile and industrial centers, only a few, such as Lyons, exhibited the characteristics of a full-fledged factory system. Small enterprise was still the rule, and in many areas this took the form of the domestic or "putting-out" system which was tenaciously resisting its inevitable extinction at the expense of the increasingly impoverished cottager.[44] In Paris itself, the great economic, as well as political and cultural, center of France, there was by no means a predominance of that large-scale industrial capitalism which flourished at Lyons. In 1851, only 7,000 Parisian *patrons* employed more than ten workers, while 32,000 independent entrepreneurs worked alone or with a single assistant.[45] It was in this milieu of small shopkeepers, master artisans, and skilled workers that Blanqui played out his political career, and from this atmosphere that he drew his intellectual nourishment.

The picture of capitalist accumulation as a reward for individual thrift and abstinence or, in Blanqui's eyes, as the illicit gains of hoarding would have had a considerable correspondence to the Parisian scene, especially before the advent of the Second Empire. Whatever his relative importance in the over-all development of capitalist accumulation, the tight-fisted, hard-working entrepreneur who had financed his rise from the masses by saving and self-denial must have been a familiar figure in the Paris of the 1830s and 40s. Blanqui named his model of capitalist rapacity "Gobseck," after Balzac's fictional usurer and fanatical

[43] Clapham, *The Economic Development of France and Germany*, p. 54.

[44] H. Sée, *Histoire économique de la France* (Paris: Librairie Armand Colin, 1942), II, 172.

[45] *Ibid.*, p. 170.

miser—a man "personifying the power of gold." [46]   Indeed, Balzac's remarkable universe contained many figures of the capitalist as the self-made man—the ex-artisan, or laborer, who has attained wealth through penury and native shrewdness. Grandet, the master cooper risen to fantastic affluence; Cesar Birotteau, the retail perfumer and Chevalier of the Legion of Honor; Goriot, who began as a workman in a vermicelli factory and amassed a fortune, were for Balzac, and probably for Blanqui, the personifications of capitalism.

Another element peculiar to French, and especially Parisian, economic life apparently influenced Blanqui's conception of capitalism. This was the dramatic predominance of the great banking houses in the economic and political life of France in the first half of the nineteenth century. According to Henri Sée:

Under Louis Philippe, what one called the *haute banque* dominated the financial world, *haute banque* so strongly characterized by the powerful dynasty of the Rothschilds. . . .[47]

The great bankers of mid-century France did not yet fulfill the credit functions of late nineteenth-century finance capitalism. Their sphere of activity was primarily government finance and speculation in public securities, more in the tradition of the Fuggers than in that of the Morgans.[48] The French economy with its combination of extensive *petit bourgeois* enterprise and tremendously powerful high finance was the background for Blanqui's theory of capitalist accumulation in terms of personal underconsumption and his personification of capitalist power in the image of the wealthy usurer.

[46] H. Balzac, "Gobseck," *The Short Novels of Balzac,* tr. K. P. Wormely (New York: The Dial Press, 1948), p. 32.

[47] Sée, *Histoire économique,* II, 229-30.

[48] P. H. Emden, *Money Powers of Europe in the Nineteenth and Twentieth Century* (London: Sampson Low, Marston and Co., Ltd., 1937), p. 378.

The identification of capitalism in general with usury has often been combined with the image of the usurer as a Jew to equate anticapitalism with antisemitism. This tendency has never, to my knowledge, been imputed to Blanqui, but there is definite evidence in his writings of a kind of leftist antisemitism which was a familiar nineteenth-century phenomenon.

It has been observed that *petit bourgeois* insecurities under the pressure of an expanding capitalist system have been focused against the middlemen and money lenders with whom the shopkeeper and artisan directly deal. For many reasons, including the historic economic situation of the Jews in Europe, the particular hostility of the "little man" toward finance capital was often manifested as antisemitism.[49] In France especially, where banking was of such great importance, and with Rothschild the exemplar of the capitalist,[50] the identification between capitalist and Jew pervaded the entire radical movement. From Fourier and Proudhon, even to the earliest issues of Benoît Malon's *Revue Socialiste* in the 1880s, runs the thread of socialist antisemitism.[51] The extent of this attitude might be in-

[49] See The description of the atmosphere in pre-Nazi Germany by F. Neumann, *Behemoth,* (New York: Oxford University Press, 1944), p. 122: "Jews occupying primarily intermediary positions were, so to speak, the concrete manifestation of capitalism for the old and new middle classes."

[50] See H. Arendt, *The Origins of Totalitarianism* (New York: Harcourt Brace and Co., 1951), p. 37. "To the small shopkeeper, the banker appeared to be the same kind of exploiter as the owner of a big industrial enterprise was to the workers. . . . Many of the bankers were Jews, and even more important, the figure of the banker bore definite Jewish traits for historical reasons. Thus the leftist movement of the lower middle class, and the entire propaganda against banking capital, turned more or less antisemitic, a development . . . of great significance in France."

[51] R. F. Byrnes, *Anti-Semitism in Modern France* (New Brunswick: Rutgers University Press, 1950), I, 114-25, 156-58, 167-78.

dicated by the observation of one scholar of the subject, that her "efforts to find sympathetic references to the Jews in French socialist literature from St. Simon to the date of Drumont's first appearance, have been futile." [52]

The authors of two influential antisemitic works were, at one time or another, political associates of Blanqui. The Fourierist, Alphonse Toussenel, who published a violently antisemitic work, *Les Juifs rois de l'époque* in 1845,[53] was an active member of Blanqui's club, the *Société républicaine centrale,* in 1848.[54] Much closer to Blanqui was Gustav Tridon, the trusted second in command of the Blanquist conspiracy during the 60s, who wrote an anti-semitic extravanganza, *Du Molochisme juif,* which was one of the most important pieces of antisemitic literature to appear in France before Drumont's *La France juive* (1886).[55]

Brief remarks scattered through Blanqui's notes are evidence of the same tendency in the master. Capitalists are personified as "Rothschilds" [56] or "Shylocks." [57] Usurious practices are described as "jewish procedures," [58] and a usurious market as "free in the judaic sense of the word, since the victim himself takes the role of solicitor." [59]

One does not wish to read too much into phrases which may reflect verbal conventions rather than prejudice. However, Blanqui's manuscripts contain the somewhat more explicit and even brutal characterization of the Jews as:

[52] Z. Szajkowski, "The Jewish St. Simonians and Socialist Anti-Semitism in France," *Jewish Social Studies,* IX (Jan., 1947), 60.

[53] A. Toussenel, *Histoire de la féodalité financière, les juifs rois de l'époque* (Paris: Gabriel de Conet, 1847).

[54] Wassermann, *Les Clubs de Barbès et de Blanqui,* pp. 96-98.

[55] R. Byrnes, *Anti-Semitism in Modern France,* p. 157.

[56] Blanqui, *Critique sociale,* II, 100.

[57] *Ibid.,* I, 189.   [58] *Ibid.,* II, 291.   [59] *Ibid.,* I, 152.

the type, the ideal, and the incarnation of swindling, usury, and rapacity. They are the horror of the nations because of their pitiless cupidity, as they had once been because of their hostility and war to the death against the human race.[60]

This is the strongest of several attacks on Jews as embodying the worst aspects of capitalism. To be fair to Blanqui one must point out that the reference to the Jews in the above quotation is in the context of an attack on all of the monotheistic sects, of which he believed Christianity to be the worst. The criticism of Judaism from the standpoint of atheism is neither racist, nor does it single out Judaism as a more detestable religion than the other Western creeds. Furthermore, Blanqui deplored religious intolerance, and wrote, for example, that the massacre of the Jewish colony of fifth-century Alexandria was an "irreparable loss" to the city.[61]

The fact remains that Blanqui's economic theories led him to identify Jews as a group with the worst practices and defining attributes of capitalism; [62] this furnishes an example of the effect which faulty economic theory had upon his estimation of the real distribution of social power. He recognized and described the contemporary facts of monopoly, overproduction, polarization, and imperialism; but he could not, on the basis of his definition of capital, interest, and exchange, understand the nature of industrial capitalism, or fully apprehend, even in his own period, the changing political consequences of economic developments.

[60] Blanqui MSS, 9587, p. 305.

[61] Ibid., 9590 (part 2), p. 499.

[62] Karl Marx also characterized the Jews as a peculiarly bourgeois and rapacious group, e.g., "Money is the jealous God of Israel, by the side of which no other god may exist." K. Marx, "On the Jewish Question," Selected Essays, tr. H. J. Stenning (New York: International Publishers, 1926), p. 92.

CHAPTER FIVE

Socialism and the Revolution

A CONDEMNATION OF capitalism is not equivalent to an affirmation of socialism. Nor do socialist aspirations combine with direct political action necessarily imply a proletarian socialist movement. Blanqui has often been characterized as an "ultra-Jacobin" whose so-called socialism was merely the expression of an extremist brand of revolutionary republicanism which manifested neither a specifically proletarian orientation nor any appreciation of the nature of the class struggle. Sometimes Blanqui is described as a socialist who was a revolutionary only in the context of nineteenth-century political oppression, but no more than a social reformer on the rare occasions when democratic political institutions gave him the opportunity for peaceful legal agitation.

In the *Encyclopédie Socialiste* of 1912, for example, we find Blanqui characterized as the personification of revolutionary zeal but credited with little or no socialist orientation. He was distinguished from the advanced democrats of his time, not by his conception of the Revolution— "Blanqui was before all a democrat and partisan of the democratic lay Republic"—but by his zeal and fidelity to the Revolution.[1] More recently, Max Nomad, in his book, *Apostles of Revolution,* has observed that Blanqui staked his life on the overthrow of the monarchy and the Church, but employed socialist ideas only as a stimulus for the

---

[1] C. Rappaport, *La Révolution sociale,* Vol. IV of *Encyclopédie Socialiste,* ed. Compère-Morel (Paris: Aristide Quillet, 1912), p. 197.

masses.   Once the Third Republic had been established
there was nothing left for Blanqui but "slow progress and
confidence in the good intentions of the politicians." [2]

These observations and others like them elicit the questions: Was Blanqui a socialist in any modern sense of the
term?   Was he a revolutionary socialist as well as a political
revolutionary?   Was his "socialism" based upon any conception of class conflict, or was it merely a rather extreme
brand of bourgeois radicalism?

WAS BLANQUI A SOCIALIST?

No one can deny that Blanqui did identify himself as a
socialist, but it is possible to quote statements in which he
gave "socialism" such broad connotations as to make it
seem no more than a synonym for justice or democracy.
When all taxes, direct or indirect, are described as applica-
tions of communism,[3] or when a socialist is defined as a
"true republican . . . a republican who is not a royalist and
a democrat who is not aristocratic," [4] a type of socialism is
evoked which seems indistinguishable from moderate
middle-class liberalism.

Blanqui's constant preoccupation with mass enlightenment as the prerequisite of the good society often seemed
to place socialism in such a distant perspective as to appear
no more than a pious reformist hope.   Communism had to
wait upon the triumph of universal public education because it could not work as long as there remained the
ignorant to be bilked by the greedy.[5]   Thus the longed-for
revolution itself would not establish a communistic economy until a fully educated people had freely decided for

[2] M. Nomad, *Apostles of Revolution* (Boston: Little, Brown and Co.,
1939), p. 74.

[3] Blanqui MSS, 9581, p. 61.   [4] *Ibid.*, p. 50.

[5] Blanqui, *Critique sociale*, I, 184-87.

it.[6]   This, Blanqui assumed, they would do inevitably.   In these passages the attainment of socialism appears more like an educationist's millenium than a revolutionary's objective.

At times Blanqui's political action seemed to correspond to gradualist social theory.   This was especially the case during those periods in which he was able to carry on legal agitation at meetings and in the press.   Even during the turbulent days of '48, when Blanqui was universally recognized as the leader of the most extreme revolutionary elements in Paris, he exhibited considerable concern for purely democratic, rather than socialist, political goals.

For example, the manifesto which Blanqui's club directed to the Provisional Government during the first week of March, 1848, carried a list of demands almost entirely in the bourgeois-democratic tradition.   The only specifically proletarian emphasis among the demands for complete freedom of speech, press, and association were the articles of the manifesto attacking the old anti-union laws and demanding that all unemployed workers be organized into a national guard.[7]

In a toast for a workers' banquet which was scheduled for sometime in the winter of 1848 (that is, after the decisive defeat of the Paris radicals), Blanqui proposed the suspension of direct revolutionary action and projected the inevitable victory of the proletarian cause through the spread of ideas.   The toast ended with the most un-Blanquist peroration: "To Victory through the word." [8]

At his trial in 1849 for conspiracy to overthrow the National Assembly on May 15, 1848, Blanqui insisted that

[6] *Ibid.,* pp. 208-12.
[7] *Les Murailles révolutionnaires* (Paris: J. Bry [Aîné], 1852), pp. 586-87.
[8] Blanqui MSS, 9581, pp. 143-45.

he would have accepted the authority of any fairly elected national legislature no matter how reactionary its composition. His bitter resistance to a premature application of universal suffrage was but a manifestation of his belief that once applied it became the sacred and inviolable expression of popular sovereignty. "From the moment that the National Assembly was convoked, I had only one role to play, that of a man of discussion." [9]

Of course his statements on this occasion may have been colored by a desire to stay out of prison, but there is corroboration of his relatively peaceable intentions, on May 15, at least, in the testimony of hostile witnesses at his trial.[10] However, one cannot conclude that Blanqui had repudiated all revolutionary activity under the Second Republic merely because he rejected the attempt to overthrow the National Assembly on May 15. One can observe that, upon occasion, Blanqui seemed willing to operate within the framework of the short-lived bourgeois democracy of the Second Republic.

During his brief periods of freedom under the Third Republic he once again left considerable evidence for the impression that in the political context of a relatively democratic secular republic he was closer to the values of a Herriot than to those of a Marty.

On the very day of the collapse of the Second Empire the Blanquists published a pledge of loyal support for the new bourgeois Government of National Defense.[11] At a meeting of his club on September 12, 1870, Blanqui argued against the demands for immediate, fundamental social

[9] *Le Moniteur Universel*, April 3, 1849.

[10] For a more detailed discussion of his participation in the events of May 15, see pp. 150-52 below.

[11] Reprinted in the published collection of his articles: Blanqui, *La Patrie en danger*, pp. XXIX-XXX.

change through an attack on capitalism. With the Prussian at the gates of Paris the issue was not, for him, collectivism or individualism, but life and death.[12] When it soon became apparent to Blanqui that the Government of National Defense was rather lukewarm in its defense of Paris, he assumed a revolutionary orientation as a patriotic obligation. He had, however, no intention of converting a patriotic war into a civil war if it could have been avoided in the best interests of France.

Even after he had been imprisoned by the Third Republic for, in his opinion, having been too good a republican,[13] he continued to follow with passionate interest the struggle to broaden democratic institutions.

Shortly before his release in 1879 he wrote a letter to Clemenceau, then the spokesman for the extreme left in the Chamber of Deputies. In this former "Blanquist of the second rank," who was neither a socialist nor a Communard, Blanqui saw the "sole hope" of the Republic. He urged Clemenceau to break away from the parliamentary parties of the left and strike out independently on a truly republican program of amnesty for the Communards, real freedom of speech and of the press, anticlericalism, and antimilitarism. There was not a reference to socialism in the entire letter.[14]

During this period Blanqui accepted electioneering and parliamentary activity as an avenue of legitimate political endeavor for the Blanquists. He himself was almost elected to the Chamber of Deputies by a Bordeaux constituency in 1879. His candidacy was initiated and pressed by a national movement of young radicals who, by and large, campaigned

[12] Reported in the issue of the journal, *La Patrie en danger*, Sept. 15, 1870.

[13] *La Gazette des Tribunaux*, Feb. 17, 1872.

[14] Geffroy, *L'Enfermé*, II, 188-98.

for Blanqui as the oldest and most faithful fighter for the republic.[15]   Although he was not seated in the Chamber, the relative success of his campaign resulted in the amnesty which released him from prison to conclude his long career in legal agitation.   Throughout this last year and a half he spoke frequently to large crowds, corresponded with many young radicals, and published a newspaper; but, as far as we know, completely eschewed conspiratorial or directly revolutionary activity.[16]

The issues most emphasized by Blanqui during the final period were: the struggle against clericalism, the attack on the standing army and advocacy of a national militia,[17] and the campaign for amnesty of the imprisoned Communards.   He encouraged radical organizations to nominate "truly popular" candidates for office,[18] planned a campaign against all existing restrictions upon universal suffrage,[19] and defined the "force of the left" as "the freedom of the tribune with France for the audience." [20]

In all of this there appears very little revolutionary socialism.   If there were no other evidence to the point one might well conclude that Blanqui was a political revolutionary who thought of socialism as a vague aspiration or a lure for proletarian support, and formal democracy as the sole end of revolutionary endeavor.   However there are a great many writings and speeches from every period of Blanqui's political life which express a commitment to

[15] This is the burden of an electoral poster, "Blanqui," pasted in the Blanqui MSS, 9593, p. 180.

[16] Geffroy, *L'Enfermé*, II, 206.

[17] The military program was the subject of the last pamphlet published during Blanqui's lifetime. L. A. Blanqui, *L'Armée esclave et opprimée* (Paris: Imprimerie du Passage de L'Opera, 1880).

[18] E.g., Blanqui's "Letter to the Citizens of Amiens," in the Blanqui MSS, 9593, p. 85.

[19] Blanqui MSS, 9593, p. 24.   [20] *Ibid.*, p. 34.

fundamental economic and social change through the violent triumph of the proletarian protagonists of the class struggle. A net assessment of the record would seem to place Blanqui squarely in the van of the struggle for a proletarian revolution.

In 1834, Blanqui published a statement of policy in the first and only issue of his newspaper, *Le Libérateur*. At this time he advocated a basic social change in which the form of government would figure "not as an end but as a means." "We call ourselves republicans," he wrote, "because we hope for a social transformation from the Republic. . . . if the Republic betrayed this hope we would cease to be republicans." [21]

A year later Blanqui and a certain Hadot-Desages circulated a handbill, titled *Propagande démocratique,* which projected the clandestine publication of a series of republican brochures.[22] In this pamphlet Blanqui's purpose was again outlined as fundamental social change. The extension of political rights through electoral reform and universal suffrage was described as a desirable means to a higher end:

the end for us is the equal distribution of the burdens and benefits of society—it is the complete establishment of the reign of equality. . . . Without this radical reorganization, all modifications in the forms of government would only be illusions, all revolutions merely comedies played for the profit of a few ambitious people.[23]

The same ideas appear in the papers of the Society of Families, presented in evidence at the trial of Blanqui and the other members of this organization in 1836. The fol-

[21] Quoted from a hand-written copy of *Le Libérateur* dated Feb. 2, 1834, which appears in the Blanqui MSS, 9592 (part 3), pp. 1-13.

[22] Apparently no brochures were ever published.

[23] Blanqui et Hadot-Desages, *Propagande démocratique* (Paris: Imprimerie de L. E. Derhan), p. 1.

lowing excerpts from the catechism of neophyte revolutionaries indicate the goals of the organization and give an
impression of the intellectual flavor of the movement:

> What is the people?
> The people is the mass of citizens who work.
> What is the fate of the proletariat under the government of
> the rich?
> Its fate is the same as that of the serf and the Negro, its life is
> only a long tale of hardships, fatigue, and suffering.
> Must one make a political or a social revolution?
> One must make a social revolution.[24]

Blanqui denied under oath that he had written the
statutes or the catechism of the society,[25] but whether he
had written them or not, as the leader of the organization
he certainly must have accepted the sense of its pronounce-
ments.

He carried these aspirations with him into the maelstrom
of 1848. On March 22 of that year, he wrote a manifesto
to the democratic clubs of Paris in which he once more
observed that the Republic would be a fraud if it merely
reflected a constitutional change. For him "the Republic"
had to be defined as, "the emancipation of the workers, the
end of the regime of exploitation. . . . the advent of a new
order which will liberate labor from the tyranny of
capital." [26]

According to Blanqui, the socialists of '48 were the only
true heirs of the glorious Jacobin "Mountain of '93," because only the socialists appreciated that the great strength
of the Mountain came from its "intimate alliance with the
Paris proletariat." [27] Indeed the bourgeois revolutionaries
had destroyed themselves by ignoring the needs of the

24 *La Gazette des Tribunaux,* Aug. 3, 1836.
25 *Ibid.,* Oct. 19, 1836.
26 Blanqui MSS, 9581, p. 116.   27 *Ibid.,* pp. 1-2.

masses. Surveying the wreckage of the revolutionary movement in November of 1848, Blanqui concluded, "A revolution must at all costs assure work and bread to the people
within twenty-four hours." [28]

One of Blanqui's most powerful affirmations of his commitment to revolutionary socialism is in a letter he wrote
to the republican exile, Maillard, in 1852.[29] We remember
that Blanqui had identified *La République* with social
emancipation. Here he equates *La Révolution* with socialism. "What is the Revolution if it is not the amelioration
of the fate of the masses?" [30] The people, he feels, will rise
only if a very specific meaning is given to "the Revolution"
—this meaning could only be found in a "war on the rich,
or, in a word, socialism." [31]

Blanqui continued with an angry critique of Mazzini's
invidious treatment of "socialist materialism," [32] which apparently had influenced the young Maillard. Mazzini's
sacred "liberty" was as much an appeal to material interests
as any other goal because liberty is a material benefit.
Actually bread and liberty are a single interest because
"hunger is slavery." Modern workers were serfs who had
been given the counterfeit of liberty amidst the real misery
of economic servitude. Blanqui concluded that no one
could be a true revolutionary without being a socialist.[33]

He held fast to this position throughout his years of
prison and plotting under the Second Empire, continuing
to insist that a viable revolution ought to carry the hope of

[28] *Ibid.,* p. 146.
[29] Blanqui's letter to Maillard is reproduced in Dommanget, *Blanqui à Belle-Ile,* pp. 177-89.
[30] *Ibid.,* p. 172.   [31] *Ibid.,* p. 185.
[32] There is an interesting chapter on the relationship between Mazzini and socialism in G. D. H. Cole, *Socialist Thought, The Forerunners 1789-1850* (London: MacMillan and Co., 1953), pp. 281-89.
[33] Dommanget, *Blanqui à Belle-Ile,* pp. 186-88.

new social rights [34] and thus would have to be made for
"the profit of labor against the tyranny of capital." [35]   He
was certain that all hope for freedom within the institutional framework of capitalist exploitation and clerical
education was no more than a Utopian dream.[36]   Consequently, he continued to organize conspiracies for the
avowed purpose of social revolution.

The political oppression of the Second Empire was met
by Blanqui with implacable defiance, but after the political
revolution of 1870 and the civil war of 1871 he seemed to
eschew insurrectionism for peaceable agitation in the framework of middle-class democracy.   Despite his campaign to
broaden democracy under the Third Republic, however,
the old intransigent did attack that "English liberty of the
individual" as the liberty of slaveholders.   He even urged
that the word "democracy" be repudiated because it had
been dishonored through use as a technique of oppression.[37]
His great objective remained progress through association
toward "communism or collectivism," if not universally,
then at least in France.[38]

To grasp the full significance of Blanqui's apparent
republicanism after 1871, of his letter encouraging
Clemenceau to fight for the Republic, and of his speeches
urging labor groups to support "truly republican" candidates, one must be aware of his peculiar definition of *La
République*.   We recall that in 1848, he had defined the

[34] Blanqui MSS, 9590 (part 2), p. 333.

[35] Quoted from L. A. Blanqui, "Instructions pour une prise
d'armes," *Archiv für die Geschichte des Sozialismus und des Arbeiterbewegung*, XV (1930), pp. 270-300.   This passage was published in
French with an introduction and notes by Georges Bourgin from a
portion of the Blanqui MSS, 9592 (part 1), pp. 32-86.

[36] Blanqui, *Critique sociale*, II, 133.

[37] Blanqui MSS, 9592 (part 3), p. 276 (dated 1880).

[38] From a speech quoted in *Ni Dieu Ni Maître*, Dec. 12, 1880.

Republic as the "emancipation of the workers"; [39] in the 1870s he asserted that the Republic was the "full amnesty of the Communards" and the "introduction of the social question into the order of the day." [40]

Obviously Blanqui's affirmation of *La République* is a sort of political mystique. The republic is not merely a type of constitutional organization; it is the equivalent of the good society. Therefore the Third Republic was not necessarily *La République,* but only a way station in a political advance which might easily be checked or reversed —especially by the subtle maneuvers of the ubiquitous monarchists. As far as Blanqui was concerned the existing government of the Third Republic (in 1879 and 1880) was, in values and in intentions, monarchistic.[41] The so-called "Moderate Republicans" were actually monarchists in disguise,[42] and even Gambetta's anticlerical Opportunists were but the contemporary equivalents of Lafayette and Dumouriez, "that is to say monarchists with a patriotic mask." [43] These observations necessarily followed Blanqui's a priori insistence that the *bourgeoisie* could never, in fact, be truly republican.[44]

These ideas led Blanqui to the sincere conclusion that the republican politicians were committed to the reestablishment of the monarchy. In 1880, for example, he was certain that Jules Grévy, the President of the Republic, was plotting to overthrow it.[45] This expectation of counter-revolution helps to explain his last publication, *The Army,*

[39] See p. 90 above.
[40] Blanqui MSS, 9594, pp. 653-54.
[41] See his speech quoted in *La Réforme* (Lyons), Oct. 21, 1879.
[42] Blanqui MSS, 9594, p. 649.
[43] Blanqui, *L'Armée esclave et opprimée,* pp. 22-23.
[44] Blanqui MSS, 9594, p. 709.
[45] *Ibid.,* 9592 (part 1), p. 34.

Enslaved and Oppressed, a pamphlet which brought some rather odd arguments to bear in favor of the establishment of a national militia in place of the standing army.[46] Why he should have mustered so much enthusiasm for this scheme is indicated by notes he penned prior to its publication.

In June of 1876, he observed that the only force possessed by the government was the army which must, therefore, "be wrested from its grasp." This so-called "republican" standing army was actually the last hope of the monarchists and only its destruction could save the Republic from monarchist plots.[47] Therefore Blanqui's last few relatively peaceable years were devoted to a verbal attack upon the forces of the inevitable counterrevolution—a counterrevolution prepared by a republican government which was in truth the "foyer of monarchism." [48]

It is true that Blanqui did not return to conspiracy as a preparation for the day of conflict, but one cannot therefore assume that he had eschewed revolutionary socialism in the relatively democratic atmosphere of the Third Republic. The Republic, as he understood the term, did not exist, and the existing forms of republican organization were soon to be assaulted by all the forces of reaction including the liberal *bourgeoisie.* The measures he adopted under these circumstances may conceivably be interpreted as products

[46] Blanqui argued, among other things, that a militia would be joined enthusiastically by local youths so long as they were not required to leave their cantons in peace time; that this system would repeat the successes it gained for the ancient Greeks and Romans; and that it would be undefeatable in a defensive war.

The basic idea is not so different from the conception of a "New Army" advanced many years later by Jean Jaurès. Cf. J. Jaurès, *L'Armé nouvelle* (Paris: Publications Jules Rouff et Cie., 1911), *passim.*

[47] Blanqui MSS, 9593, pp. 13-19.

[48] Quoted from a speech to the electors of Lyons in 1879, in *Ni Dieu Ni Maître,* May 1, 1881.

of a gradualist philosophy, or simply of exhaustion and old age, but are perfectly intelligible as expedient tactics for a socialist, or ever a revolutionary, movement, given his interpretation of the political situation.

On the 27th of December, 1880, five days before his death, Blanqui answered a crowd's cheers for the tricolor by an affirmation of his loyalty to the red flag alone.[49]

It is clear that Blanqui fought for something other than capitalist democracy and that the goals of his revolutionary endeavor included some sort of egalitarian and collectivist economic system. However, he lacked the theoretical equipment to define clearly his "socialism" and was not interested in making an analysis of the social order which did more than define its injustices, flay its defenders, and predict the conditions of its destruction.

THE THEORY OF THE CLASS STRUGGLE

Still it might be argued, especially from a Marxist viewpoint, that Blanqui remained a Utopian or Jacobin democrat to the degree that he ignored the historical struggle between economic classes in his revolutionary program. Many have accepted Lenin's flat dictum, "Blanquism is a theory that denies the class struggle." [50]   On the other hand, Maurice Dommanget (who has an unrivaled command of the material relating to Blanqui as well as an almost unrivaled sympathy for him) holds that Blanquism and

[49] Described in *Ni Dieu Ni Maître*, Jan. 2, 1881. The persistence of his old insurrectionist values is indicated in a letter written to a friend, Dr. Susini, in 1880. "Whenever I revolted I was impelled by the most imperious and sacred duty. I greatly fear that the baseness of Opportunism imposes this duty upon us again." Quoted in Dommanget, *Blanqui*, p. 44.

[50] V. I. Lenin, "K Itogam S'ezda," from *Sochineniia* (3d ed., Moscow: Giz, 1935) IX, 237. This is a speech, "The Congress Summed Up," dated 1906.

Marxism had "the same conception of the evolution of the world in terms of the class struggle." [51]

From what he considered to be an orthodox communist viewpoint André Marty also declared that Blanqui's "highest merit" lay in his early recognition of the historical necessity of the class struggle.[52] Marty was attacked in the periodical, *Cahiers du Communisme,* by Roger Garaudy on precisely this issue. Garaudy cited Blanqui's famous statement at his trial in 1832 that he was a "Proletarian . . . one of thirty million Frenchmen who live by their labor" as evidence, not of a theory of the class struggle as the motor of history, but of the unsophisticated Babouvist dichotomy of "rich and poor." Blanqui's "proletariat" was only the equivalent of the "people" of eighteenth-century *petit bourgeois* rationalism.[53]

Roughly the same interpretation was advanced by the historian Arthur Rosenberg who pointed out that Blanqui's thirty million proletarians would have made up ninetenths of the French population in 1832, and embodied but a tiny fraction of a true industrial proletariat—that Blanqui belonged in the democratic tradition which thought of the proletariat in the classic Roman sense of the vast undifferentiated mass of the unwealthy and underprivileged.[54]

Statements which appear to validate this interpretation can be found in Blanqui's writings. Especially does his apotheosis of "the people" have the flavor of the eighteenth century. "The people" is the supreme tribunal before

[51] M. Dommanget, *Blanqui à Belle-Ile,* p. 12.

[52] A. Marty, *Quelques Aspects de l'activité de Blanqui,* p. 8.

[53] R. Garaudy, "Le Neó-blanquisme de contrebande et les positions antiléninistes d'André Marty," *Cahiers du Communisme,* Jan., 1953, p. 39.

[54] A. Rosenberg, *Democracy and Socialism,* p. 31.

which all ideas must be aired; [55] "the people" is the pow-
derkeg which is someday to explode; [56] "the people" has a
thirst for truth and a need for encouragement.[57]

Nevertheless there is considerable material which shows
that Blanqui's idea of "the people" contains implications
beyond the vague democratic dichotomy of "the many and
the few." His writings and speeches evince a theory of
economic classes more precise and more sophisticated than
the one implied by his self-identification as a "Proletarian
. . . one of thirty million Frenchmen."

As early as 1831, Blanqui evoked the question of class
conflict in letters to a friend who was apparently a moderate liberal. In these letters he referred with great bitterness to the *"bourgeoisie"* who had crawled out of their
caves to reap the fruits of the July Revolution, and who
now wished to hang the heroes of those "three glorious
days." The "republicans" made the error of laying aside
their arms after winning the victory and, as a consequence,
now faced the bayonets of "the government of the bourgeois classes." [58] His correspondent's hope of slow progress
based upon the gradual reconciliation of class interests was
chimerical because the *bourgeoisie,* jealous of its new-found
power, was determined to hurl the masses back into bond-
age. Therefore, a more frightful and evenly matched revolution than that of '89 was inevitable.[59]

Blanqui's description of the struggle for the political
spoils of the July Revolution is quite ambiguous. His correspondent is not informed precisely what the "bourgeois

[55] Blanqui MSS, 9590 (part 2), p. 399.

[56] *Ibid.,* (part 1), p. 173.

[57] *Ibid.,* 9584 (part 1), p. 119.

[58] Letter from Blanqui to Mlle Montgolfier dated July 19, 1831, in
Les Lettres, Aug., 1906, pp. 447-49.

[59] Letter from Blanqui to Mlle Montgolfier dated July 18, 1833, in
Les Lettres, Sept. 1906, p. 513.

classes" are, nor is there a description of the class composition of the republican forces which the *bourgeoisie* have
begun to attack. This ambiguity was again manifest at the
trial of 1832 where, as Garaudy and Rosenberg have observed, the "Proletariat" with which Blanqui identified
was the equivalent of the poor and oppressed. The reforms which the young firebrand advocated at this trial go
along with his vague democratic alignment. They included the demands for universal suffrage, a fairer tax system, and a patriotic war of popular liberation.[60]

There are, however, ideas expressed at the same trial
which contain the germs of a fairly sophisticated theory of
historical development based upon the conflict of economic
and social classes. Blanqui briefly outlined the concept of
a change from the conflict between the *bourgeoisie* and the
feudal aristocracy to a new struggle between the proletariat
—"the last form of slavery"—and the temporarily ascendent
middle class: "It appears to me that here, under new forms
and between other adversaries is the war of the feudal
barons against the merchants whom they plundered on the
high road." [61]

These ideas were applied to an interpretation of the
Revolution of 1830 in a speech which Blanqui drafted in
1832 for a meeting of the republican society, the Friends of
the People.[62] This begins, "it is unnecessary to hide the
fact that there is a war to the death between the classes
which compose the nation." The three contending "interests" were, the *élevé* (that is, the aristocracy), the *classe
moyenne ou bourgeoisie,* and *le peuple.* Their relation-

---

[60] *Défense du citoyen Louis Auguste Blanqui devant la Cour d'Assises 1832* (Paris: Imprimerie de Auguste Mie, 1832), *passim.*
[61] *Ibid.,* p. 6.
[62] Blanqui MSS, 9592 (part 3), pp. 17-26.

ships had become crucial to the political history of France since 1815.

The middle class had withdrawn its support from Napoleon because his ambitions ultimately had a bad effect on business. It was willing to share the control of the nation with the old aristocracy and consequently accepted and supported the Charte of Louis XVIII and the government of the Restoration. After 1827, Charles X, in alliance with the Jesuits, began an offensive against the *bourgeoisie*. A deadly struggle broke out between the "government, supported by the nobility, clergy, and great landowners," and the middle class. In the ensuing battle, the people, hating the Bourbons, were launched against the dynasty of the *bourgeoisie*. After their victory the politically immature and leaderless masses left the field to the rich parliamentarians who had been trembling between the Scylla of the monarchy and the Charybdis of the triumphant people.

The supreme betrayal of the people had been in the installation of King Louis Philippe.[63] The new administration, faithful to its class origins, had been characterized by its hatred and cruelty toward the workers. In fact it was moving into an alliance with its old enemies on the Right in order to assure its domination over the exploited majority of the nation. Henceforth one could expect a bitter war between the people and the bourgeois-aristocrat alliance.

This analysis of history as class struggle does not define in economic terms the social categories of "bourgeois" and

[63] According to Heinrich Heine, who was present when this or a similar speech was delivered to a meeting of the Society of Friends of the People on February 2, 1832, Blanqui, in words full of "wit, honesty, and anger," characterized Louis Philippe as *la boutique incarneé*. H. Heine, *French Affairs, Letters from Paris,* tr. C. G. Leland (London: W. Heinemann, 1893), I, 82.

"proletarian" whose conflict was to decide the political configurations of the future.   There is a somewhat clearer
statement of the economic relationships among the contending classes in articles drafted in 1834 for Blanqui's
short-lived newspaper, *Le Libérateur*.   This journal was
dedicated to "the exploited workers" and was to carry out
an analysis of "the relationship which exists today between
master and man, the social question which virtually constitutes the entire problem of political economy." [64]

In a draft for an article which never appeared in the
paper, Blanqui distinguished between "slavery and privilege" in modern society on the basis of the ownership of
"the instruments of labor." [65]   The enslaved masses, deprived of the instruments of their labor, were at the mercy
of the minority which controlled them.   It had been difficult for the proletariat to identify its oppressors as every
attempt had been made to obscure "the duel to the death
between profit and wages."   When, as at Lyons in 1834,
the flagrant antagonisms of class interests permitted no
more illusions, the workers arose as one man to fight their
oppressors.[66]

Blanqui by no means identified the entire radical and
revolutionary movement with the proletariat.   When he
and his archenemy Barbès were prisoners on Belle-Isle in
the 1850s, they became the leaders of two irreconcilable
factions among the political prisoners.   Blanqui proudly
wrote that all former ideological lines were blurred in this

[64] Blanqui MSS, 9592 (part 3), p. 3.

[65] Garaudy remarks: "From the economic point of view, Blanqui is
the first to envisage class relationships from the point of view of production and not of distribution."   R. Garaudy, *Les Sources françaises
du socialisme scientifique* (Paris: Editions Hier et Aujourdhui, 1948),
p. 234.   We might add that this is the case in spite of the fact that
Blanqui's economic analysis is based upon distribution rather than
production.   See Chap. IV above.

[66] Blanqui, *Critique sociale*, II, 123-24.

conflict as the real workers, and those sons of the middle class who truly identified with the proletariat, rallied round himself, whereas Barbès became the leader of the "bourgeois" elements exclusively.[67]

In his letter to Maillard in 1852,[68] Blanqui vigorously criticized the former's attempt to repudiate any invidious distinction between "bourgeois" and "proletarian" revolutionaries and to identify himself solely as a "democrat." Words like "democrat," Blanqui asserted, served to obscure those real social and political differences which reactionaries preferred to disguise. "They do not desire that the two opposed camps be called by their true names: Proletariat, Bourgeoisie." Blanqui had now a precise conception of the two camps and proceeded to define them for Maillard's benefit:

The middle class comprises most of the individuals possessing a certain amount of wealth and education, financiers, merchants, proprietors, lawyers, doctors, bureaucrats, rentiers—all those living on their revenues and the exploitation of the workers. Add to these a fair number of landowners who have wealth but not education and you will have a maximum number of no more than four million. There remain thirty-two million proletarians without property, or with very little property, and living only by the product of their hands. It is between these two classes that the bitter war has arisen.[69]

Clearly, Blanqui's "thirty-two million proletarians," roughly eight-ninths of the French population in the 1850s, would still have included a small proportion of industrial

[67] In a letter to Eduard cited in Dommanget, *Blanqui à Belle-Ile*, pp. 59-61.

[68] See p. 91 above.

[69] Quoted in Dommanget, *Blanqui à Belle-Ile*, p. 170. In Turgot's remarkable analysis of class relationships we find a similar characterization of the class of "simple artisans, who own nothing but their muscles, and profit only by their daily labor." Quoted in L. Cahen, "L'Ideé de lutte des classes au XVIIIe Siècle," *Revue de synthèse historique*, XII (Jan.-June, 1906), 51-52.

workers and an overwhelming majority of those *petit bourgeois* elements which Marx considered essentially reactionary [70]—the peasant proprieters, petty functionaries, shopkeepers, and self-employed artisans, who, after all, were
"the people" evoked by any good Jacobin.

Yet Blanqui's "proletariat" is no longer equivalent to
"the people" of the eighteenth-century reformers.   This
honorable title he now bestows upon "the class of workers"
to distinguish them from the "third estate." [71]   When he
applies this distinction to an analysis of contemporary political conflict, and especially when he relates it to control
over the instruments of labor he has come quite close to
the Marxian conception of class.   However, the Soviet historian, Volgin, has correctly observed that the clearest distinction made by Blanqui is between the class which lives
by exploitation and the class which supports itself without
exploiting others.[72]   This is by no means the same as the
basic Marxian dichotomy between the swelling mass of
wage laborers and the dwindling number of those who
reap the surplus value of the workers' industry through
their control over the means of production.

Whether or not Blanqui's conceptions of class struggle
anticipated modern socialist theories, they did define the
nature of socialist action for him.   A feeling for the relationship between economic classes and political power was
the basis of his rejection of reforms which had to be carried out in a society presenting opportunities for economic

[70] Cf. Marx and Engels, "Manifesto of the Communist Party," *Selected Works* (Moscow: Foreign Languages Publishing House, 1950),
p. 42.

[71] Blanqui MSS, 9592 (part 1), p. 306.

[72] In V. P. Volgin's introduction to L. A. Blanqui, *Izbrannye
proizvedeniio*, tr. F. B. Shuvayef (Moscow: Academy of Sciences SSR,
1952), p. 38.

exploitation. Private property, the institutional expression of an initial usurpation of the fruits of the earth, guaranteed the continued existence of a predatory society which nullified piecemeal ameliorations.

Historically, the ruling classes had consolidated the benefits of economic spoilation by a system of law based upon the "right of property"—a right which, in the eyes of the capitalists, transcended and determined all other rights.[73] The values of contemporary society were the needs of its exploiters. "Freedom" meant the freedom to exploit; the freedom of the market, of the commercial jungle; the freedom of the worker to toil and starve.[74] "Order" and "moderation" meant the meek and sheeplike acceptance of the interests of their rulers by the masses.[75]

Blanqui observed that years of political reform and even revolution had never shaken Capital's control of the sources of power, nor could he envision the voluntary abandonment of this power under any conceivable circumstances. Indeed, the rich would no more be inclined to relinquish peaceably their privileges than had been the nobility to give up their feudal rights.[76]

Limited economic reforms, such as redistribution of the great estates,[77] had no more chance than constitutional reforms to liberate the masses so long as the State remained the "gendarmerie of the rich against the poor," [78] and the Church and press, the servants of capitalism. Foreign policy, like domestic politics, was only a reflection of the class interests of the rich and a technique of class domination—

[73] Blanqui, *Critique sociale*, II, 118-19.
[74] *Ibid.*, I, 152, 188.
[75] Blanqui, *La Patrie en danger*, p. 137.
[76] *Défense du citoyen Louis Auguste Blanqui . . .*, p. 9.
[77] Blanqui, *Critique sociale*, II, 107.
[78] *Ibid.*, p. 146.

"no matter what the fate of the nation, the Bourse will live on." [79]

When Blanqui wrote that the social question could only be considered after the most forceful and irrevocable solution of the political question,[80] he did not mean that social ends were secondary to the attainment of political democracy,[81] but that political power had to be wrested from the groups whose interests were antithetical to fundamental social reform. We remember that he saw ignorance as the progenitor of economic misery and social injustice and felt the source of progress to be the communication of thought. But there could be no legal avenue to mass enlightenment so long as the laws were framed and executed by the minority which profited from the ignorance of the people.[82] The mind of the nation was held in thrall by the combined forces of capital, the army, and the Church [83]—it could only be liberated by force.

The revolution was to provide this force, not for the creation, but for the liberation of the socialist future. That is, it was not to dictate the future to the people but free them to work it out for themselves [84]—to prepare the soil for the harvest of a socialist posterity.[85] A revolution thus embodied more than the assurance of physical liberation from political and social oppression. The very ideas for an improved organization of society could not be apprehended until a "social upheaval" had torn the veils from the future [86] and enabled men to discover the new society

[79] Blanqui, *La Patrie en danger,* p. 227.
[80] Blanqui MSS, 9591 (part 2), p. 70.
[81] Cf. Nomad, *Apostles of Revolution,* p. 72.
[82] *Défense du citoyen Louis Auguste Blanqui* . . . , pp. 8-9.
[83] Blanqui, *Critique sociale,* II, 351.
[84] Blanqui MSS, 9590 (part 1), pp. 158-59.
[85] *Ibid.,* p. 420.   [86] *Ibid.,* 9583, p. 391.

among the ruins of the old.[87]   The revolutions of 1830 and
1848 had, for example, released a spate of socialist theories
in France.[88]   These tentative steps on the path of intellectual progress were checked by the barrier of bourgeois society—"a barrier which only the hand of the Revolution
can break." [89]

BLANQUI AND THE UTOPIANS

Blanqui's hostility to much contemporary socialist theory
sprang in part from his belief that the conception of the
new social order was frozen in the old. Since it was impossible to envision the configurations of the future until
a revolution had destroyed the past, it was manifestly ridiculous to draw up the blueprints for a postrevolutionary
society.

One of our most grotesque presumptions is that we barbarians,
we ignoramuses, pose as legislators for future generations. Those
generations, for which we take the trouble to feel concern and
prepare the foundations, will render us a hundred times more
pity than the caveman inspires in us, and their compassion will
be a great deal more reasonable than ours.[90]

Naturally the defenders of capitalism always demanded
from the socialists a complete and foolproof model of the
society for which they fought. Actually the socialist need
not be ashamed because he carries no blueprints in his
pocket. It is enough that he demonstrate the flaws in the
existing order, condemn it, and destroy it.[91]   Capitalist
quibbles over a hypothetical socialism always mask the
crudest self-interest. When the bourgeois economists ask,
"Who will empty the chamber pot in Utopia?" what they
really mean is, "Who will empty my chamber pot?" [92]

[87] *Ibid.*, 9581, p. 162.   [88] *Ibid.*, 9583, p. 39.
[89] *Ibid.*, 9581, p. 162.
[90] Blanqui, *Critique sociale*, I, 143.
[91] *Ibid.*, II, 113.   [92] *Ibid.*, I, 191-93.

As a matter of fact, the capitalists have no cause for complaint about a lack of socialist formulae. The Fourierists, St. Simonians, Comtists, communists, and even the anarchists have all long since drawn up the plans for their model prisons, "where humanity will revel in its perfect shackles." [93]

One is not surprised to discover Blanqui's hostility toward the so-called Utopian Socialists. To him they were the fanatical devotees of preconceived ideas which had had nothing but pernicious effects on the mind of the French workman. His devastating comment on the projects of Cabet was typical:

Communism . . . is not an egg which can be laid and hatched in a corner of the world by a two-legged bird without wings or feathers.[94]

Communism was inseparable from revolution, and the "charms of Utopia" only helped to lead socialists from the necessary path of political action.[95] The Fourierists and St. Simonians, with their ridiculous assurances that the usurpers of power will voluntarily renounce it, and their attempts to end the bad effects of usury without destroying the economic foundations of interest,[96] were in practice quietists or counterrevolutionaries. The manufacture of "Utopian digressions" while the people starved was virtually a murderous practice, especially since the Utopians would much prefer to see society remain in its present savage state than accept the tiniest deviation from the fulfillment of their own particular plans.[97]

[93] *Ibid.*, II, 113.
[94] Blanqui MSS, 9590 (part 1), p. 373.
[95] *Ibid.*   [96] *Ibid.*, 9581, p. 90.
[97] Blanqui, *Critique sociale*, II, 116.

The proof of the pudding for the old streetfighter was in the concrete political programs and the personal careers of the Utopians. Fourier, for example, whose schemes were developed from false psychological assumptions and at worst could furnish material for an alienist, ended by assigning an important role and a share of wealth to the capitalists in his essentially conservative Utopia.[98] His disciples, as well as the Comtists and St. Simonians, had all eventually declared war on the revolution and become pillars of the Second Empire, perfectly at home among the speculators, soldiers, and clerics of a particularly reactionary regime.[99] All of them were guilty of the supreme iniquity of attempting to establish intellectualized religions which were actually pitiful parodies of Catholicism.[100]

Characteristically, Blanqui was not entirely consistent in his hostility toward his socialist rivals. Previous to the 1860s he apparently looked upon all socialists with a sort of eclectic benignity. In the letter of 1852, chiding Maillard for a lukewarm attitude toward socialism, he went so far as to assert that even the most pacifistic reformers are essentially revolutionary if they support socialism. One could appreciate their anticapitalism while rejecting their temperament.[101] The idea that a common rejection of capitalist institutions was a satisfactory basis for socialist unity

[98] Blanqui MSS, 9590 (part 1), pp. 186-89. Blanqui based his rejection of Fourier's theory of innate and constant instincts upon a conception of change (see p. 44 above), which may well have been derived from Hegel: "the entire development of terrestrial things is accomplished through the law of opposites, perpetual and imperceptible change, the progressive mutation of ideas." *Ibid.*, p. 187.

[99] Blanqui, *Critique sociale*, I, 200.

[100] Blanqui MSS, 9592 (part 1), p. 492, and *ibid.*, 9590 (part 1), pp. 165-66.

[101] In Dommanget, *Blanqui à Belle-Ile*, p. 188.

is implied by Blanqui's oft-quoted observation on Proudhonism and Communism:

Communism and Proudhonism argue vigorously on the bank of a stream over whether there is a field of corn or wheat on the other side. Let us cross first, we will see when we get there.[102]

Blanqui had, throughout most of his life, a great deal of respect for Proudhon. The latter returned this, at least to the point of admiring Blanqui's sincerity and pitying his fate. However, Proudhon felt that Blanqui's political tactics were foolish, hopeless, and perhaps the emanations of a mind destroyed by too many years in prison.[103] Their fundamental differences were gradually borne upon Blanqui until he had moved from a position of considerable admiration to that of rather acidulous criticism of Proudhon.

In 1848, Blanqui praised Proudhon as a powerful orator and thinker who was one of the finest hopes of the future republic and one of the best soldiers of the people.[104] Nineteen years later, looking back on that period, he still felt that he and Proudhon, despite their theoretical differences, were *frères ennemis* under the banner of socialism since they agreed upon the crucial conception of the illegitimacy of interest. Unfortunately, Proudhon's disciples had rejected this idea—the one conception that had made their master "a true socialist"—and had actually set up usury as their God and capital as their sovereign.[105]

[102] Blanqui, *Critique sociale*, II, 314-15.

[103] For scattered remarks to this effect: P. J. Proudhon, *Lettres au citoyen Rolland*, ed. J. Bompard (Paris: Éditions Bernard Grasset, 1946), pp. 84-85 (Letter dated June 13, 1860), pp. 134-35 (Letter dated March 16, 1861), pp. 142-43 (Letter dated April 7, 1861). P. J. Proudhon, *Les Confessions d'un révolutionnaire* (Paris: Au bureau du journal La Voix Du Peuple, 1849), p. 33. P. J. Proudhon, *La Révolution au XIXe siècle* (Paris: Garnier Frères, 1851), p. 3.

[104] Blanqui MSS, 9581, p. 306.

[105] Blanqui, *Critique sociale*, II, 149-50.

The tremendous gulf between his own ideas of class struggle and violent revolution and Proudhon's essentially antirevolutionary and anticommunist theory was inevitably brought home to Blanqui when he began to observe the political consequences of Proudhonism. He became especially bitter against the various programs of the Proudhonists during the period of the formation and early history of the First International, which he at first believed to be a stalking horse for the French government.

The very powerful French section of the International was originally composed of trade-unionists who were greatly influenced by Proudhon's ideas for mutual credit societies and cooperatives and hostile to any form of direct political action.[106] For several years Blanqui identified the International with its French section and attacked it as a counterrevolutionary organization established to propagate the Proudhonian panaceas of Tolain, Fribourg, and the other French leaders.[107]

Blanqui characterized their programs as "pure economism"—a rejection of the political and religious questions which were inseparable from the struggle for proletarian emancipation. Any program for social justice in the framework of a society based upon capitalist economics and subjected to clerical exploitation was but a Utopian dream. Furthermore, the specific reforms of the Proudhonists, especially credit societies and cooperatives, were based upon saving and interest-taking, the distinguishing elements of capitalist enterprise. The worker was lured into essentially capitalist operations in which the church-inspired ignorance of the great mass would set it off from the intelligent minority which would come to dominate the organization

[106] J. L. Puech, *Le Proudhonisme dans l'Association Internationale des Travailleurs* (Paris: Félix Alcan, 1907), pp. 151-62.
[107] Blanqui, *Critique sociale*, II, 135-67.

and assume the role of a worker aristocracy. Naturally, the government favored a movement which skimmed off the cream of the proletariat, turning the natural leaders of the working class into a new, more rapacious *bourgeoisie*.

Therefore, Blanqui forbade his followers to attend meetings of the International, and when some of them disobeyed him at Geneva in 1866 they were expelled from the Blanquist organization.[108] When he learned of the eventual defeat of the French section of the International at the Congress of Basle in 1869, he celebrated it as a triumph of communism which had thrown fear into the ranks of the *bourgeoisie*. However, he felt that there was ultimately little hope in the International which was hemmed in by an imperceptible circle of ambitious factions and "illusions of organization." Its vacillating policies would furnish no sure leadership for the masses and, in fact, only reflected the progress of popular opinion without contributing to that progress.[109]

Blanqui's continuous quarrel with the theories and tactics of Proudhon's disciples apparently led him to reconsider the contributions of his old comrade in arms. In the late '60s he began to find all sorts of sophistries, equivocations, and even "Jesuitism" in Proudhon's writings which he could only excuse as manifestations of senility.[110] He finally summed up Proudhon as a revolutionary who was, temperamentally at least, eager to destroy the *status quo*, but whose theoretical heritage was a "labyrinth without issue, which now serves as a grove of academe, for his pacific disciples." [111]

108 Da Costa, *Les Blanquistes*, pp. 18-20.
109 Blanqui MSS, 9591 (part 2), pp. 362-63.
110 *Ibid.*, 9590 (part 1), pp. 222-24.
111 *Ibid.*, 9592 (part 3), p. 259.

Blanqui thus explicitly divorced himself from the great tradition of French socialism which is loosely called "Utopian." He was, indeed, greatly influenced by the Utopians —especially by the economic and historical ideas of St. Simon—but, historically, he stands in a completely different tradition. This is the political and social tendency which one might characterize as Jacobin Communism, if "Jacobin " is taken to indicate something like the spirit of 1793 rather than a specific political grouping. His theoretical socialism and practical revolutionism are the joint products of this tradition.

CHAPTER SIX

The Tradition of Jacobin Communism

THE FUSION OF complete devotion to a theoretical *Égalité* with uncompromising political activism, which we have called Jacobin Communism, has had a virtually continuous influence on French radical politics since 1792. This tradition of ruthless violence and humanitarian zeal has run from the revolutionary days of the *enragés* and the *Hébertistes,* through Babeuf and his disciples, as an element in Carbonarism and the early republican movement, down to the exponents of revolutionary syndicalism, and is probably carried on by certain elements of the French Communist party today. Blanqui was its most characteristic, and its most faithful, adherent.

A notable tendency of the ideology which develops out of this tradition is its Frenchness—its intellectual parochialism and passionate patriotism. These attributes were certainly not monopolized by the Blanquists in nineteenth-century France but their influence upon Blanquist ideology was of the greatest importance. Blanqui never really belonged to that supranational community of leftist exiles which was such an important element in the radical movements of the nineteenth century. Except for a few years in Belgium in the 1860s, and possibly a week or so in Spain, England, and Italy, Blanqui was in prison or in Paris or on his way to prison or Paris during most of his long political career.

Blanqui habitually wrote a short commentary on what he was reading, and these brief notes show that he read widely and not only in French sources.   However, there can be little doubt that the major influences upon his philosophy, social theory, and even economic theory were, aside from the classics, predominantly French.   His political ideas and tactics, too, were derived from French precedents and worked out in reference to the specific French political situation.   His polemic was directed almost exclusively against Frenchmen—against the Positivists, against Bastiat, against Proudhon and the French section of the First International, against Thiers and the other leaders of the French *bourgeoisie.*

One must qualify these observations to note that Blanqui was at least cognizant of many of the foreign leaders of European radicalism.   There are, among his notes, favorable references to Lassalle,[1] and hostile criticism of Lassalle's German rival, Schulze-Delitzsch, whose cooperatives and credit associations looked to the Frenchman like the stalking horse of German capitalism.[2]   There are bitter diatribes against the liberal nationalists, Mazzini, Garibaldi (before 1870),[3] O'Connell,[4] and Louis Kossuth.[5] There are quotes from the writings of Heine [6] and Herzen,[7] and one or two cryptic references to Bakunin.[8]   And there is considerable evidence that Blanqui was more familiar with Marx and Marxism than is commonly supposed.

[1] Blanqui MSS, 9590 (part 1), p. 8; 9587, p. 14 (dated 1863).

[2] *Ibid.,* 9590 (part 1), pp. 9-10, and Blanqui, *Critique sociale,* II, 168-69.

[3] See p. 119 below.

[4] Blanqui MSS, 9590 (part 1), pp. 31-33.

[5] Quoted in Dommanget, *Blanqui à Belle-Ile,* p. 185.

[6] Blanqui MSS, 9592 (part 3), p. 365.

[7] *Ibid.,* p. 287.

[8] *Ibid.,* 9591 (part 2), p. 451 (dated 1868).   Bakunin's name appears on a list of potential sympathizers and enemies in case of a revolution. It is also found in a letter from a Blanquist listing contacts outside of France.   *Ibid.,* 9594, p. 429.

We know that Marx was quite familiar with Blanqui's career and had a qualified admiration for the French communist.[9] It is almost certain that the two men never met,[10] but they had common political associations as early as the 1840s when Marx became acquainted with the members of the German League of the Just,[11] some of whom had fought under Blanqui in the Paris insurrection of May, 1839.[12] Marx was in Paris in March and part of April in 1848, and was, for a short period, active in one of the radical clubs where he advanced substantially the same arguments on the issues of elections, taxes, and the composition of the National Guard, as those delivered by Blanqui from the tribune of his Central Republican Society.[13] Whether Blanqui met, or knew anything about, the young German orator at the Society of the Rights of Man remains in the realm of conjecture.

Some of the Blanquists who fled to London after 1848 collaborated with Marx in the formation of the Universal

[9] Marx more than once referred to Blanqui as "the head and the heart of the proletarian party in France," quoted in Garaudy, *Sources français du socialisme scientifique*, p. 217. On the other hand, Marx criticized the type of conspiratorial tactics favored by the Blanquists in the harshest terms. See A. Cornu, *Karl Marx et la Révolution de 1848* (Paris: Presses Universitaires de France, 1948), pp. 62-63, also B. Nicolaievsky and C. Maenchen-Helfen, *Karl Marx*, tr. G. David and E. Mosbacher (Philadelphia: J. B. Lippincott Co., 1936), pp. 214-15.

Engels, of course, ultimately condemned Blanquism as completely outmoded adventurism. See pp. 135-36 below.

[10] In 1879 Lafargue wrote to Blanqui, "Marx . . . would be very happy to make your acquaintance." Blanqui MSS, 9588 (part 2), p. 678.

[11] Nicolaievsky, *Karl Marx*, pp. 79-80.

[12] F. Engels, "History of the Communist League," in *Germany: Revolution and Counter Revolution* (New York: International Publishers, 1933), pp. 120-21.

[13] S. Bernstein, "Marx in Paris, 1848: A Neglected Chapter," *Science and Society*, III (Summer, 1939), pp. 347-55.

Society of Revolutionary Communists [14] and described
their efforts in letters to the imprisoned Blanqui.[15] The
London coalition was shortly dissolved with some bitterness,[16] but Marx remained in friendly communication with
several Blanquists throughout the 1850s and 1860s, and
continued to follow Blanqui's career with interest and sympathy.[17]

    There are positive indications that this was a two-way
relationship. In 1864, for example, the Blanquist Dr. Wat-
teau writes to his master Blanqui that he had sent Tridon's
book *Les Hébertistes* to Marx per Blanqui's request.[18]
Much more important links between the two leaders were
Marx's sons-in-law, Charles Longuet and Paul Lafargue,
who were both strong friends and admirers of Blanqui.
Lafargue especially transmitted mutual compliments back
and forth across the channel, writing to Marx from France
in 1869, "Blanqui has the greatest esteem for you," [19] and
in 1879, writing from London to Blanqui, "Marx, who has

14 N. Plotkin, "Les alliances des Blanquistes dans la proscrition,"
1848, *Revue des Révolutions Contemporaines* (Dec., 1951), pp. 119-21.
    15 Blanqui MSS, 9581, p. 206. A letter from Barthelémy dated July
4, 1850.
    16 Nicolaievsky, *Karl Marx,* pp. 218-19.
    17 When Blanqui's controversial *Avis au Peuple,* a letter which at-
tacked other French radicals, appeared in London (see p. 169 below),
Marx defended it enthusiastically and had copies of it smuggled into
Germany. See Karl Marx/Friederich Engels, *Historisch-Kritische
Gesamtausgabe* (Berlin, 1931), Dritte Abteilung, Band I, p. 168 (Letter
from Marx to Engels dated March 8, 1851); p. 191 (Letter from Marx
to Engels dated May 3, 1851).
    18 Blanqui MSS, 9592 (part 2), p. 146.
    19 Marx/Engels, *Gesamtausgabe,* Dritte Abteilung, Band 4, p. 159.
Quoted in a letter from Marx to Engels dated March 1, 1869. Blanqui
also conveyed his thanks to Marx, through a mutual friend, for the
sympathy of the German proletariat during his trial in 1861. Marx/
Engels, *Gesamtausgabe,* Dritte Abteilung, Band 3, p. 25. Mentioned
in a letter from Marx to Engels dated June 9, 1861.

followed your political career with great interest, would be very happy to make your acquaintance." [20]

More important for our purposes is the evidence of Blanqui's familiarity with Marx's thought. In 1869, Marx wrote of a report from Lafargue to the effect that Blanqui was very enthusiastic about Marx's "Poverty of Philosophy" and was lending it to all of his friends.[21] There is an interesting little note in the Blanqui manuscripts defending *Das Kapital* against a hostile review which appeared in *La Revue Positiviste* in 1869.[22]

Blanqui, the omnivorous reader, almost certainly read the first of these works and possibly the second, but it is difficult to establish evidence of a direct Marxian influence upon his ideas.[23] He was very sympathetic to foreign socialists whom he considered to be sincere revolutionaries but apparently continued to take his intellectual sustenance almost exclusively from French sources.

PATRIOT OR CHAUVINIST?

Blanqui's whole life was colored by that French patriotism which distinguished him from the many cosmopolitan expatriates among his fellow radicals. Born into the Napoleonic age, he never forgot the sight of foreign troops marching into that territory which his father had helped

[20] Blanqui MSS, 9588 (part 2), p. 678.

[21] Marx/Engels, *Gesamtausgabe,* Dritte Abteilung, Band 4, p. 159.

[22] Blanqui MSS, 9590 (part 1), p. 64. The reviewer, Raberty, argued that even though capitalist profits might be an undeserved appropriation of labor value, they were necessary for the expansion of modern industry. Blanqui remarked that Raberty was merely observing that exploitation was necessary for the capitalist, and, in these terms, the issue would ultimately be resolved in favor of the stronger—that is, in favor of the workers.

[23] Garaudy, however, believes that Blanqui was deeply influenced by Marxism, at least after 1869. Garaudy, *Les Sources français du socialisme scientifique,* p. 254.

to bring into the French Republic.[24]   As a young agitator he subscribed to the aggressive nationalism of his French contemporaries and dreamed of the fourteen armies which France might raise once more to hurl upon the "Europe of Kings," not of course, "to regain its absurd conquests," but to free it from foreign control.[25]   Toward the end of his career Blanqui became relatively pacifistic as the dangers for the workers of mass warfare grew more apparent,[26] but he never relinquished his passionate French patriotism.

   To some, Blanqui patriotism was one of his most significant qualities.   Alexandre Zévaès titled his biography of the revolutionary, *Auguste Blanqui, patriote et socialiste français,* and wrote in his conclusion:

from Blanqui we retain the memory and the lesson of his vibrant, ardent, and clairvoyant patriotism which never, even in the blackest hours, despaired of the destiny of France or doubted its inevitable recovery of its world mission.[27]

Blanqui virtually redeemed himself in the eyes of many French conservatives by his fierce, agonized, and brilliant newspaper articles on the siege of Paris during the Franco-Prussian War.[28]   He was, as we have seen, prepared to subordinate his political ends to unity in the face of the enemy but not to support any government which contemplated surrender to the hated Prussians.   His rage was directed against the half-hearted defenders of the capital and the "barbarian hordes" [29] which had appeared before it.   Later

[24] Blanqui MSS, 9581, pp. 175-76.

[25] *Défense du citoyen Louis Auguste Blanqui . . . ,* p. 12.

[26] By 1880 Blanqui was certain that war was never desired by the working class.   Blanqui, *L'Armée ésclave et opprimmée,* p. 28.

[27] Zévaès, *Auguste Blanqui,* p. 247.   Cf. J. Jaurès, *Oeuvres,* ed. Max Bonnafour (Paris: Les Éditions Rieder, 1931), III, 421.

[28] See the eulogy of Blanqui's patriotism by the conservative journalist J. J. Weiss in the *Paris Journal,* Feb. 18, 1872.

[29] Blanqui, *La Patrie en danger,* p. 19.

generations of Frenchmen were to delight in Blanqui's characterization of the Germans as ruthless beasts dedicated to the destruction of the Latin race.

Blanqui had actually felt these sentiments long before the invasion which evoked such a fierce expression of them. By 1866, this relentless enemy of the French government was following Bismarck's successes with increasing suspicion and fear. He remarked then that the Prussians, who were not a nation of citizens, but a "troop of slaves," had hurled themselves upon the German peoples like a horde of Tartars.[30]

The Germans were not the only object of Blanqui's nationalist antipathies. England, the classic home of capitalist exploitation,[31] with its deplorable climate, language,[32] and women,[33] was especially to be censured for the terror and oppression visited upon the colonial peoples by the Anglo-Saxon race.[34] He did, however, credit England with a magnificent literature and a relatively equitable legal system. He also felt that the very intensity of capitalist exploitation in England endowed it with a high revolutionary potential.[35]

[30] Blanqui MSS, 9591 (part 2), pp. 496-97.

[31] Blanqui, *Critique sociale,* II, 207.

[32] Blanqui MSS, 9581, p. 16. Blanqui expressed his dislike for the gallicization of certain English words: "Club-cloub!-cleub!—Ah! yes, cleu-eu-eu-eub! . . . Are we going to substitute for the pure, simple, brief accent of our clear language the intonations of English mewing?"

[33] *Ibid.,* 9584 (part 1), pp. 95-97. An exiled friend is warned not to choose an Englishwoman for a wife, as they were the personification of *"pot-au-feu* and domestic egoism."

[34] Blanqui, *Critique sociale,* II, 73. Blanqui condemned colonialism and nineteenth-century ideas of white superiority. However, he was affected by the racist theories of his era. The whites, he admitted, might be more intelligent than the colored races, but this was a compensation for innate white ferocity and cruelty. "The negroes . . . sweeter, gayer, and more tender," had less need of an intelligence to act as the checkrein of a natural ferocity. Blanqui MSS, 9581, pp. 283-84.

[35] *Ibid.,* 9592 (part 3), pp. 23-26.

The United States, which was a republican Valhalla to many nineteenth-century European radicals, was treated somewhat less favorably by Blanqui. It was, he felt, a land of great personal fortunes [36]—a nation whose social problems had been resolved by the existence of free land. When the free land ran out, predicted Blanqui, an upheaval of the greatest violence would occur, because "the Anglo-Germanic race is infinitely more egotistical and unsociable than ours." [37]

The independence movements of oppressed nationalities received little sympathy from Blanqui if they smacked at all of clericalism, antisocialism, or hostility to France.[38] Italian nationalism was especially guilty of these sins. Mazzini, the notorious antisocialist, manifestly envied France her "intellectual and political superiority" and tried to make Europeans forget that she had "emancipated mankind." [39] Even Garibaldi (who was to receive effusive praise after serving France against Prussia in 1870, and endorsing Blanqui's candidacy in 1879) [40] was, in the 1860s, described by the Frenchman as the "fierce enemy of everything which bears the French name." [41] Both men came from Nice, and as Blanqui pointed out, they had gone in opposite directions. Consequently, he rejected all requests to serve with the One Thousand in Sicily and characterized the entire movement of the Risorgimento as superstitions, priest-ridden, incurably bourgeois, and, worst of all, implacably anti-French.

The examples of Blanqui's extreme nationalism should

[36] *Ibid.*, 9590 (part 1), p. 278.
[37] *Ibid.*, 9592 (part 3), pp. 68-69.
[38] The cultural nationalism of the Flemish, Magyars, and Slavs he dismissed as the "pretentions of tribes and clans." *Ibid.*, 9581, pp. 19-20.
[39] Quoted in Dommanget, *Blanqui à Belle-Ile,* p. 180.
[40] E.g., Blanqui MSS, 9592 (part 3), p. 272.
[41] *Ibid.*, 9584 (part 1), p. 112.

not blind one to the fact that the revolutionary had spurned the tricolor to embrace the red flag. He was too much of a socialist to adhere consistently to a narrow nationalism. At least once in his writings he invoked the world struggle of the international proletariat against the capitalists of every country. In a projected proclamation to the French army he specifically mentioned the toilers of Germany and England as having the same interests as the French worker and the same enemies. "The workers of all nations are brothers and they have but one enemy, the oppressor who forces them to kill each other on the fields of battle." [42]

There is a rather interesting passage on the Crimean War in Blanqui's notes which indicates that he did not commit himself to the French cause under all circumstances in the manner of a Barbès. [43] In Blanqui's eyes the war which France was fighting in 1854 against the citadel of European reaction was particularly unfortunate for his cause. Because France was basically a "country of chauvinists," the war threatened to end all effective resistance to the tyranny of Louis Napoleon. [44] A victory for Bonaparte was a victory for despotism and consequently a victory for Russia. Before the Tsarist hordes could overrun the East, revolutionary Europe would have to be destroyed, and Napoleon III was doing Russia's work in France just as his uncle had done before him. "Russia actually won the battle of Austerlitz." The result of the Bonaparatist victory at Sevastopol might be the Russianization of France. [45]

[42] Blanqui," Instructions pour un pris d'armes," *Anchiv fur die Geschichte des Arbeiterbewegung*, XV (1930), pp. 299-300.

[43] On the occasion of the Crimean War, Barbès wrote a patriotic letter to George Sand which came to Louis Napoleon's attention. As a result of this, Barbès was pardoned and released from prison over his own protests. J. A. Barbès, "Notice sur la vie d'Armand Barbès," *La Révolution de 1848*, II (1905-6), p. 214.

[44] Blanqui MSS, 9584 (part 1), p. 72.

[45] *Ibid.*, 9581, pp. 346-48.

The question which should most concern us is not the precise intensity of Blanqui's patriotism but the nature of its relationship to his peculiar brand of revolutionism. Blanqui was so narrowly a *French* revolutionary because of the special revolutionary role he envisioned for France. Like so many of his contemporaries, Blanqui believed that his native land had a mission of world leadership, not as a conqueror, but because it uniquely embodied the highest aspirations of mankind.[46]   France, whose dynamic spirit had already destroyed its own moribund traditions and contributed so greatly to the liberation of other peoples,[47] was the bearer of that "principle of equality" destined to conquer the nations.[48]

This attitude would seem to imply considerably less concern with the long-run revolutionary possibilities of universal social and economic developments than with the immediate potentialities of the French political situation. The world proletariat was to awaken at the sound of the tocsin in the streets of Paris.   Therefore, the more reactionary the French regime, the heavier the responsibility of Frenchmen immediately to overthrow it.   The French socialists could not await the fruition of slowly maturing universal forces because they themselves carried the seed of the world revolution.

All Frenchmen who devoted themselves to human progress were, for Blanqui and many others, but the executors of the testament of the great Revolution and at the same time its heirs. The certainty that political violence was a legitimate, honorable, and peculiarly effective mode of social change was the essence of Blanqui's political patri-

---

[46] See C. J. H. Hayes, *The Historical Evolution of Modern Nationalism* (New York: The Macmillan Co., 1948), pp. 156-57.

[47] Blanqui MSS, 9590 (part 1), p. 262.

[48] Blanqui, *Critique sociale*, II, 126-27.

mony.   In this he was no different than all of those Frenchmen, from neo-Babouvists to Bourbons, who defined their
various political commitments in terms of the politics of
the Revolution of 1789.[49]   Blanqui, too, made some attempt to define his own ideology by relating it to the
aspects of the seminal revolution.[50]

THE INFLUENCE OF THE PAST

We are not surprised to discover that Blanqui did not
indiscriminately admire the great figures of the revolutionary era.   If he was a son of the Revolution, he was certainly
no heir of Lafayette, the Girondists, or even, he tells us, of
Robespierre.   He saw among contemporary politicians
whom he most despised exact prototypes of these heroes of
bourgeois historiography.   Lafayette and Dumouriez, for
example, were reincarnated by Gambetta and his Opportunists, all "monarchists with a patriot's mask." [51]   The
Girondist tradition was particularly obnoxious to Blanqui
because of its anti-Parisian federalism.[52]   It was carried on
in the nineteenth century by Ledru-Rollin and the other
self-styled Jacobins who made up the so-called "Mountain
of 1848." [53]

   The original Mountain of 1793 had, of course, been sublime, although lacking "positive theories growing out of
analysis of the body politic."   Although they lacked a true

[49] See J. P. Mayer, *Political Thought in France* (London: Rutledge
and Kegan Paul Ltd., 1949), pp. 1-7.

[50] Zévaès writes, in reference to Blanquism: "The conception of
revolutionary power has its origins in the memories of the Revolution
. . . the Convention . . . those popular forces which had dominated
the decisive days of the 14th of July and the 10th of August . . . those
sections of the Commune which were dominated by Marat, Hérbert,
Chaumette." Zévaès, *Auguste Blanqui*, p. 147.

[51] See pp. 93-94 above.

[52] E.g., Blanqui MSS, 9581, pp. 127-28.

[53] *Ibid.*, pp. 3-4.

science of society to build upon, the old revolutionaries had yet drawn from their hearts the Declaration of the Rights of Man, "which broadly interpreted, contained the germ of all of the developments of future society." [54] Their miserable nineteenth-century epigoni in preempting and petrifying the tradition of the Declaration of Rights had destroyed its spiritual force through "the Jewish cult of the letter." Now, concluded Blanqui, the Mountain was dead and socialism was its only heir.[55]

Blanqui was not prepared to accept even the Jacobin heritage without discrimination. The tendencies associated with the name of Robespierre were broadly condemned. Blanqui's criticisms of Robespierre were put on paper only in his unpublished manuscripts, yet, as we have seen, Mathiez considered their influence to be so pervasive that he felt compelled in 1928 to publish and refute them.[56] Mathiez felt that Blanqui, like his Girondist father, applied essentially bourgeois criteria to the revolutionary situation and saw nothing in the Terror of '93 and '94 but a religious problem.[57]

Blanqui did condemn Robespierre most severely for the religiosity which he felt to be a betrayal of the revolutionary potential of pure atheism. However his criticisms are not completely based upon anticlericalism. When Blanqui wrote, "The Jacobin Club was no more than a church with Robespierre for the Grand Master," [58] he meant to attack not only Robespierre's religiosity but also what he considered to be a dangerous and hypocritical lust for personal power. Robespierre is described as a "premature

[54] *Ibid.*, p. 1. [55] *Ibid.*, p. 10.
[56] See p. 16 above.
[57] A. Mathiez, "Notes de Blanqui sur Robespierre." *Annales Historiques de la Révolution Française*, V (July-Aug., 1928), p. 319.
[58] Blanqui MSS, 9581, p. 86.

Napoleon" who knowingly sacrificed Clootz to the kings
and Chaumette to the priests of Europe in order to
strengthen his own position.[59]

Although Blanqui sometimes defended the Terror he
was appalled by its application to men like Danton and
Hébert. To the self-appointed Cicero, St. Just, men such
as Vergniaud, Chaumette, Danton, Hébert and numberless
other revolutionaries were Catilines marked for merciless
destruction.[60] Blanqui denied that he was a *Hébertiste*
because he resented the death of Chaumette any more than
he was a *Dantoniste* because he deplored the death of
Desmoulins and remarked, "It is as odious to have guil-
lotined C. Desmoulins because he was *spirituel,* as
Chaumette because he was not *spiritualiste.*"[61] This
strange "eclecticism of the guillotine" troubled and baffled
the people and ended in the popular abstention from the
revolutionary struggle.[62]

Blanqui's denunciation of the execution of revolutionaries by revolutionaries and his sorrow at what he considered to be the essentially meaningless quarrels between
such men as Desmoulins and Hébert[63] appear somewhat
odd in the light of his uncompromising rejection of all cooperation with "bourgeois revolutionaries."[64] He readily
projected the conflicts of the Revolution forward into his
own era but did not accept the harsh consequences of
theoretical divisions in the past. Although he deplored the
factional conflicts of the old revolutionaries, we have seen
that he was by no means neutral in his estimate of the factions. He bitterly condemned most of the revolutionary
leaders and had good things to write only about the
Hébertistes.

59 *Ibid.,* p. 79.   60 *Ibid.,* p. 15.
61 *Ibid.,* p. 373.   62 *Ibid.,* 9591 (part 2), p. 347.
63 *Ibid.,* 9581, p. 371.   64 See pp. 168-70 below.

If any men before the *Babouvistes* can be considered the progenitors of Blanquism, they are the zealots who poured into the Paris streets behind Hébert. Blanqui's favorite lieutenant Tridon published a work on the *Hébertistes* in 1864 which vigorously defended them against their nineteenth-century critics. There is substantial, although not conclusive, evidence that Blanqui himself drafted at least a part of the introduction to this work.[65] In the portion most probably written by Blanqui, *Hébertisme* is characterized as:

the brigand who stops despotism at the turn of the road and cries, pistol at its throat, Equality or death. . . . if it [*Hébertisme*] had the exultation which leads to victory, it lacked the *sang-froid* which conserves it.

Although he realized that "the *Hébertistes* perished through an excess of passion," the author regrets the disappearance of such heroic, disinterested figures. In words very similar to Marty's estimate of Blanquism, the critique of *Hébertisme* asserts: "But if it is good to avoid their faults, their qualities ought to serve as an example."

For Blanqui the positive quality of *Hébertisme* is devotion—devotion to that boundless aspiration which is *La Révolution*. The most visible proofs of this devotion were the close relationship with the Paris masses and uncompromising atheism.[66] Blanqui praised *Hébertisme* as the embodiment of the absolutely necessary revolutionary will,

[65] G. Tridon, *Les Hébertistes* (Paris: Chez L'Auteur, 1864). Blanqui is mentioned as the author of the introduction to this work by the Blanquist, Eudes; quoted in *Ni Dieu Ni Maître*, May 1, 1881. A portion of the introduction in Blanqui's hand is to be found in his manuscripts. Blanqui MSS, 9590 (part 2), pp. 43-47.

[66] Even the *Hébertistes* were guilty of *spiritualisme* in their worship of the Goddess of Reason, but this summation of eighteenth-century values was infinitely preferable to Robespierre's retrograde cult of the Supreme Being. Blanqui MSS, 9581, pp. 83-84.

if not the highest political intelligence. In the intensity of his own voluntarism we can discern the relationship between Blanqui's political career and his interpretation of the French Revolution.

Despite their evident sympathies the Blanquists were not neo-*Hébertistes*. Their socialism sets them off from the most extreme of bourgeois radicals and brings them into closest historical relationship with the first of communist revolutionaries—the *Babouvistes*. It is often remarked that Blanqui received a laying on of hands from Philip Buonarroti, the venerable survivor of the *Babouviste* Conspiracy of Equals and the elder statesman of French radicalism in the 1820s and 30s. This relationship is seen as a link in a continuous communist tradition extending from Babeuf and Buonarroti through Blanqui to Vaillant and Tkatchev and, according to some, to Lenin.[67]

There is evidence of a personal association between Buonarroti and Blanqui. They were both members of the revolutionary society of the Friends of the People in 1832; [68] they both appeared on the defense committee for the Lyonnais and Parisians accused of fomenting insurrection in April of 1834.[69] In 1835, Buonarroti wrote a letter in which he mentions Blanqui as a witness to certain of his actions.[70]

It is interesting to note that there is scarcely a reference to Buonarroti or *Babouvisme* in the existing writings of Blanqui. It has been conjectured that any written evidence of Blanqui's interest in *Babouvisme* was in the bundle of

[67] E.g., Dommanget, *Blanqui à Belle-Ile*, p. 7.

[68] A. G. Garrone, *Fillipo Buonarroti e i revoluzionari dell'ottocento (1828-1837)* (Turin: Biblioteca di cultura storica, 1951), p. 246.

[69] *La Gazette des Tribunaux,* May 30 and 31, 1835.

[70] This letter is published in: P. Robiquet, *Buonarroti* (Paris: Librairie Hachette et Cie., 1910), p. 238.

manuscripts which were destroyed by his mother.[71] This may be the case, but in the salvaged writings on the revolutionary period and in autobiographical material on Blanqui's political development in the 1820s and 1830s no reference to Babeuf has been found.

The nature of any relationship with Buonarroti and the extent of the influence of Babouvism upon Blanqui's ideas are therefore open questions. Virtually everyone who has written in the field does postulate some such influence.[72] The similarities in tactics, personal commitment, and certain specific ideas encourage the deduction that Blanqui must have been influenced by Buonarroti or some source of *Babouvisme*.

Ideological parallels do not establish a causal relationship between *Babouvisme* and Blanquism with absolute certainty, because they both obviously drew upon the same intellectual tradition and could have independently arrived at similar positions. However there are striking correspondences which are certainly worth remarking.

The conception of the revolutionary political role of education is a part of the eighteenth-century heritage to which Blanqui particularly subscribed. Babeuf's position on this issue was virtually identical to that of his successor and was expressed in a very similar manner. In his *Cadastre perpétuel* of 1789, Babeuf wrote, "If men had always enjoyed equal education . . . the majority would never have submitted itself to the dishonoring shackles which the

---

[71] S. Bernstein, *Buonarroti*, tr. (into French) by M. Gilles (Grandes Figures Hier et Aujourd'hui), pp. 254-55.

[72] See Garonne, *Fillipo Buonarroti*, pp. 245-50; Bernstein, *Buonarroti*, pp. 254-55; N. Stewart, *Blanqui* (London: Victor Gollancz Ltd., 1939), pp. 33-40; E. Fournière, *La Règne de Louis Philippe*, Vol. VIII of *Histoire Socialiste*, ed. J. Jaurès (Paris: Publications Jules Rouff et Cie., 1906), p. 172; G. Sencier, *Le Babouvisme après Babeuf* (Paris: Marcel Rivière et Cie., 1912), pp. 71-73.

minority has dared to impose upon it." [73]   Some seventy years later, Blanqui expressed the same meliorist optimism when he asserted that a *lycée* education for all would guarantee the reign of absolute equality.[74]

Notwithstanding their faith in reform through education, both men were passionate egalitarians who believed that social justice could only be attained when social institutions, in the words of Babeuf, "denied to everyone the hope of ever becoming either richer, more powerful, or more distinguished by his knowledge than any of his equals." [75] From this concept they both derived a commitment to basic institutional change, and communism.

These examples by no means exhaust the interesting theoretical correspondences between *Babouvisme* and the theories of Blanqui.   There are, as well, the more immediate relationships between Blanqui's ideas and the preachments of Philip Buonarroti in the 1830s.   According to Buonarroti's biographer Garrone, Blanqui's advocacy of a merciless war between the classes and his indifference to constitutional reform and to reform through the redistribution of the land are all "the doctrinal premises . . . of the egalitarianism of Buonarroti." [76]

Probably no relationship to *Babouvisme* is as important to the understanding of Blanquism as the historical fact of Babeuf's Conspiracy of Equals.   When, in 1796, the *Babouvistes* attempted to seize political power in order to force a fundamental change in economic institutions they

[73] Quoted in Dommanget, *Pages choisies de Babeuf* (Paris: Librairie Armand Colin, 1935), p. 85.
[74] Blanqui, *Critique sociale*, I, 211-12.
[75] Quoted in Dommanget, *Pages choisies de Babeuf*, p. 261.   For Blanqui's similar ideas on the role of equality, see pp. 65-66 above.
[76] Garrone, *Fillipo Buonarroti e i revoluzionari dell'ottocento*, p. 249.

established the historical precedent for Blanquism. The combination of communism and conspiracy distinguished both groups from their fellows in the French socialist movement up to 1871.

Although it might appear that the techniques of Babeuf's conspiracy served as a model for Blanqui's political tactics, there is reason to believe that the Carbonarist movement of the 1820s was probably of greater influence upon Blanquist action. We have had occasion to cite Geffroy's assertion that Blanqui's Carbonarist experiences during the Restoration were to put a decisive stamp upon his entire career.[77]

The *Charbonnerie*—the French society of the "charcoal burners"—was a typical manifestation of the well-rooted French tradition of clandestine dissent. The young intellectuals of the 1820s grafted the tactics of the Italian nationalist societies called the "Carbonari[78] onto the traditions of freemasonry, the secret workers' orders of the Compagnonnage, the clandestine groupings of the great Revolution, and the aborted conspiracies of the first years of the Bourbon Restoration.

According to most accounts Carbonarism was introduced to the French in 1820 by several young republican militants, including Bazard, who was later to share and elaborate the

[77] Geffroy, *L'Enfermé*, I, 38.

[78] The Italian movement itself may have had French roots. The charcoal-burners of eighteenth-century Franche-Comté were organized into secret *Ventes*—a *Vente* probably referring to a stand of timber. The Italian cell, or *Vendita*, may have been derived from this usage, and, in turn, *Vendita* again became *Vente* when the French took up Carbonarism in the 1820s. See J. H. Lepper, *Famous Secret Societies* (London: Sampson Low, Marstow, and Co., 1932), pp. 95, 126. *Memoirs of the Secret Societies of the South of Italy, Particularly the Carbonari* (London: John Murray, 1821), pp. 1-4.

heritage of St. Simon, and Buchez, who eventually turned from conspiracy to Christian Socialism.[79]   It was stripped of a great deal of the semi-Masonic mysticism which attended it in Italy and made into the vehicle for a compact, closely directed movement for political subversion.   The movement shortly attained remarkable popularity among young Parisians and maintained an even more remarkable secrecy as it spread throughout the schools of the city, into other towns and even into the regiments of the line in the border garrisons where, at last, the police began to get some wind of it.[80]

Carbonarism attracted some of the eminent "liberals" who led the legal opposition to the Restoration, and the conspirators depended upon peripheral sympathizers, such as Lafayette, to bring over the mass of the population upon the success of the anticipated military coups.   The history of their specific attempts does not concern us here although it is worth noting that the Carbonari managed to effect a movement of national dimensions which flowered into three almost simultaneous risings at Belfort, Saumur, and La Rochelle in 1822.[81]   The methods of the Carbonari carried them right up to the day of the rising with relative secrecy and a rather high degree of coordination, but failed them in the last hours when liaison broke down and the careless-

[79] There are several articles on the organization and personnel of French Carbonarism, with an excellent bibliography, in the journal, *La Révolution de 1848:* M. A. Calmette, "Les Carbonari en France," *La Révolution de 1848,* IX (1912-13), 401-17, and X (1913-14), 52-73, 117-37, 214-30.   Cf. L. Blanc, *The History of Ten Years* (London: Chapman and Hall, 1844), I, 48-52; Trelat, "La Charbonnerie," *Paris révolutionnaire* (Paris: Chez Guillaumin, 1834), II, 275-341.

[80] *Ibid.,* pp. 288-89.

[81] See E. Guillcn, *Les Complots militaires sous la Restauration* (Paris: Librairie Plon, 1895).

ness or treason of individuals betrayed the plans to the authorities.[82]

The methods of carbonarist organization borrowed by Blanqui will be described.[83] These technical aspects of revolutionary organization—the pyramidal structure, the isolated cells, the secret leadership—for all their importance in Blanqui's career, are no more significant than his experience of what might be called the atmosphere of Carbonarism. The unifying ideology of Carbonarism was a detestation of the Bourbon Restoration. Any ideological precision would have rendered the cooperation of militant young Bonapartists, republicans, Orleanists and neo-Jacobins impossible. The organization survived as long as it defined itself by action alone; as soon as its members began to concern themselves with theory, internal fissures were revealed which probably contributed as much as political failure to the destruction of the movement.[84] Thus, Carbonarism in its heyday was an organized *Résistance,* the members of which were set off from other opponents of the Restoration by the intensity of their commitment—commitment to direct action and commitment of personal security. Blanqui, when hardly more than a boy, made this commitment.

In a passage from the manuscripts, written in the third person but almost certainly autobiographical, Blanqui described his political baptism in the Carbonarist move-

[82] Blanqui tried to avoid last minute betrayals by leading rehearsals of the projected coup, one of which, without warning, was to become the real insurrection.

[83] See p. 158 below.

[84] Trélat, *Paris révolutionnaire,* p. 330; F. Corcelle, *Documents pour servir a l'histoire des conspirations* (Paris: Paulin, 1831), p. 12.

ment.[85]   In 1822, at the age of seventeen, he had seen the execution of the Carbonarist martyrs, the famous "four sergeants of Rochelle." Moved by their fate, he joined the Carbonari himself and vowed to avenge them.

Blanqui joined the Carbonari after it had passed its peak as an effective movement, but its activist tendencies corresponded to what he described as his dislike of theories which neglected practical action.[86]   He himself was extremely active in the student demonstrations and riots of the late 1820s, receiving his first revolutionary wounds in the *émeutes* of 1827.   By 1830 he was already cast in the mold of uncompromising activism.

In that year he was a reporter for the liberal journal, the *Globe,* but he was completely out of sympathy with the cautious, legalistic, young intellectuals who directed it.   He later described an altercation between himself and the editors of the *Globe* on the day which saw the beginning of the July Revolution.   As the revolution rumbled up into the streets, Cousin and the other editors counseled caution and loyalty to the white flag of the Bourbons.   Blanqui responded, "Arms will decide.   As for me, I am going to take up a rifle and the tricolor cockade." [87]   This he proceeded to do, only to discover that he had helped to deliver the political child of those very journalists.

When he entered the lists against the new Orleanist monarchy, Blanqui found at his side many republicans, Jacobins, and *neo-Babouvistes* who continued to conspire in the old revolutionary tradition of idealistic violence.

[85] Blanqui MSS, 9581, pp. 175-81.   This account is written in Blanqui's hand and follows a copy of a letter to Lacambre dated August, 1848.   In this letter Blanqui rejected Lacambre's suggestion that he write an autobiography, yet we can probably assume that the biographical fragment immediately following the letter was Blanqui's attempt to sketch out something of the sort in the third person.

[86] *Ibid.,* p. 177.   [87] *Ibid.,* pp. 180-81.

But by the end of the 1830s all but a handful of zealots had rejected conspiracy as impractical.[88]   There were always orators to summon up the spirit of Hébert and the Carbonari, but only Blanqui and a few kindred spirits continued to live out the extreme consequences of the revolutionary ideal.

There are many possible explanations for Blanqui's persistence in a political tradition which so many of his companions had rejected and which was to bring him so much suffering.   A partial answer is perhaps discerned in the assumptions of an absolute political morality which are implicit in a great many of his *ad hoc* political polemics. "Morality," he wrote, "is the foundation of society." [89]

Blanqui's political morality was derived from an ethos of rationally apprehended natural rights.   This is clearly shown by his characterization of the various inequities which he intended to destroy.   Lending at interest, for example, was a violation of the "social law." [90]   Land acquired by force or speculation could not be possessed "legitimately." [91]   Thus he approaches social reform, not from the nineteenth-century philosophies of utility or historical necessity, but from the eighteenth-century rationale of natural social law.

Moreover, he reasoned that the passive victim of a violation of natural rights was as guilty as his oppressor, for the acceptance of injustice was its sanction: "to submit to an illegality when one can resist it is to legitimatize it." [92] Therefore everyone was morally bound to the struggle

[88] G. Weill, *Histoire du parti républicain en France (1814-1870)* (Paris: Librairie Félix Alcan, 1928), p. 138.

[89] *Candide,* May 3, 1865.

[90] Blanqui, *Critique sociale,* II, 24.

[91] *Ibid.,* p. 47.

[92] Blanqui MSS, 9591 (part 1), p. 347.

against injustice, no matter what the cost. Any deviation from this course, any rationalization of nonrevolutionary goals, any hint of even a lukewarm resistance was, for Blanqui, a sin.

Blanqui prophesied the bitter course that his life was to take when, at his trial in 1832, he defiantly asserted the transcendent moral nature of revolutionary activity. All men of heart and intelligence were bound, even at the cost of their own lives, to call the masses up out of servitude. One must be willing to hurl himself into the chasm to make a road for the march of humanity.[93]

He not only lived up to this prescription—he made of it his métier. Blanqui was probably the first professional revolutionary, the first to have no career but the overthrow of existing institutions. Late in his life he wrote the credo which might be considered to sum up all of the virtues and defects of his career: " *Le devoir d'un révolutionnaire, c'est la lutte toujours, la lutte quand même, la lutte jusqu'à extinction.*" [94]

[93] Société des Amis du Peuple, *Procès des Quinze*, p. 80.
[94] Blanqui, "Instructions pour une prise d'armes," *Archiv fur die Geschichte des Arbeiterbewegung*, XV (1930), 277.

CHAPTER SEVEN

The Reluctant Insurrectionist

BLANQUI'S IMMOLATION on the altar of the Revolution is the most familiar aspect of his career. He is often referred to as an adherent of a sort of mindless revolutionism, a "maniac of conspiracy" [1] whose only conception of the goal and conditions of social change was the violent conquest of political power, "no matter how, no matter when, by no matter whom, provided that the ideal was a good one." [2] There is not only the record of a lifetime of conspiracy, prison, and more conspiracy to bear out this contention, but also certain of Blanqui's public statements such as the one reported by an interviewer from the London *Times* in 1879:

I have no theory. I am not a professor of politics or socialism. What exists is bad. Something else must take its place.[3]

Political thinkers fundamentally in sympathy with Blanqui's revolutionary goals have often characterized him as a naïve zealot to be admired primarily for his ardor and courage. One of the most influential estimates of Blanqui from this point of view was Engels's letter to *Der Volksstaat* in 1874 [4] embodying an attack on the "Revolutionary Commune" which the Blanquist Communards had estab-

---

[1] T. Delord, *Histoire du Second Empire* (Paris: Librairie Germer Baillière, 1873), III, 77.

[2] Ralea, *L'Idée de révolution*, p. 25.

[3] *The Times* (London), April 28, 1879.

[4] Engels, "The Program of the Blanquist Fugitives from the Paris Commune," in Marx, *The Civil War in France*, pp. 133-44.

lished in London. Engels very properly distinguished these disciples from Blanqui himself, but dismissed the old leader as a "revolutionary of the preceding generation," a political revolutionist who was socialist only through a sentimental sympathy with the sufferings of the people.

In his political activity he was mainly a man of action, believing that a small and well-organized minority, who would attempt a political stroke of force at an opportune moment, could carry the mass of people with them by a few successes at the start and thus make a glorious revolution.

Engels's definition of Blanquism has been broadened by certain writers to subsume virtually any socialist commitment to revolutionary action. This is implied in the writings of the Revisionist Eduard Bernstein who deplored the "Blanquist error" of those Marxists who tended to exaggerate "the creative faculties of revolutionary action at the expense of the socialist transformation of modern society." [5]

Lenin, of course, vigorously denied all imputations of Blanquism to Bolshevik revolutionary theory. He distinguished between the Marxist theory of the emancipation of humanity through the class struggle of the proletariat and the Blanquist faith in a conspiracy of a small minority of intellectuals,[6] and elaborated three major differences between the Marxian and the Blanquist approach to an uprising. For Marxists as opposed to Blanquists, the uprising was based on the advanced class rather than upon a conspiracy or party, it was based upon "the revolutionary upsurge of the people," and it took account of the crucial stage in the history of a maturing revolution when the action of the vanguard of the people was at its height and

[5] E. Bernstein, *Socialisme théorique et Social Démocratie pratique,* tr. A. Cohen (Paris: P. V. Stock, 1900), p. 55.

[6] Lenin, "K Itogam S'ezda," in *Sochineniia,* IX, 237.

when the enemies of the people were weakest and most divided.[7] The implication of Lenin's statement is that Blanqui lacked the conception of the necessary objective conditions of a successful proletarian revolution and an appreciation of the role of the majority of the working class in its consummation.

This viewpoint is considerably elaborated in Neil Stewart's biography of Blanqui. According to Stewart, Blanqui did contribute a great deal to the understanding of the necessary connection between socialism and political conflict.[8] He correctly foresaw the proletarian revolution and the need for an advanced party to give it direction but neglected to organize or even maintain contact with the great mass of the workers upon whom the success of social revolution must ultimately depend.[9] He almost completely neglected mass propaganda because of his certainty that the workers would automatically support a successful revolution. He was hostile to all forms of proletarian action that were not directly revolutionary because he interpreted history, not in terms of a long-run development of economic and political forces, but as the product of individual actions.[10]

NONREVOLUTIONARY TACTICS ON THE ROAD TO REVOLUTION

Even historians most favorable to Blanqui accept some measure of the criticism directed against his failure to appreciate the revolutionary potential of mass agitation or to recognize the practical limitations of conspiracy. Between this critique, however, and the characterization of Blanqui as a mindless political adventurer, there is a tremendous

[7] Lenin, *On the Eve of October*, p. 5.
[8] Stewart, *Blanqui*, p. 331.
[9] *Ibid.*, pp. 40-42.   [10] *Ibid.*, p. 328.

gulf. The conflicting interpretations of the nature of Blanqui's commitment to a revolution adumbrate some of the questions that should be raised in a study of Blanquism: Was "Revolution now" the substance of Blanquist political theory? Was insurrection the only revolutionary technique acceptable to Blanqui? What was to be the relationship between Blanqui's conspiratorial elite and the masses? Did he recognize any objective conditions for a revolutionary situation?

One might begin by introducing the evidence which makes it necessary to qualify the assertion of Blanqui's complete alienation from the masses and his absolute rejection of political tactics which were not directly relevant to insurrection. Undoubtedly he had nothing but scorn for many forms of peaceful socialist and worker activity. Especially in the period between 1848 and 1870 did he stand aside from the major activities of the French labor movement. He was bitterly critical of the mutual credit societies, worker saving associations, and cooperatives of the epoch.[11] On the other hand, he did come to feel that a revolutionary coup could only be guaranteed by a revolutionary spirit in the masses and consequently found certain long-run tactics of mass stimulation, which might or might not be directed toward immediate revolutionary ends, to be quite desirable. The techniques which he praised from time to time were electioneering, strikes, and clandestine propaganda.

Blanqui's attitude toward electioneering was extremely ambiguous. He usually repudiated the use of the ballot under those regimes which denied the use of the press or tribune to leftist organizations.[12] He was from time to

11 See pp. 109-10 above.
12 Blanqui MSS, 9581, pp. 250-51.

time willing to participate in bourgeois elections if his sympathizers could campaign without fear of immediate reprisals from the police.[13] However, Blanqui often expressed a dislike of parliamentary institutions even when they were the product of the uncoerced will of the electorate. Historically, parliaments were the concrete manifestations of the ancient resistance to a monarchial despotism, but once brought into existence they in turn became the instruments of human oppression because they were chosen by an intellectually debased electorate.[14] The years of reactionary control over the minds of the people (especially in the countryside) would bear their evil fruit no matter how fair and free the elections.[15] Therefore the radical's dream of a legislative seat was "as dangerous as it was delusive" [16] so long as the enlightened elements had not had a comparable opportunity to educate the masses.

It was from this basis that Blanqui developed his well-known arguments against the application of universal suffrage immediately after a revolution. The majority which could be marshalled on the side of the reactionaries because the free dissemination of ideas had been so long suppressed was not a majority of citizens, but a troop of slaves. "It is a blind tribunal which has for seventy years heard only one of the two parties. It ought to hear the other side of the case for seventy years also. Since they were not able to plead together they will plead one after the other." [17]

One might conclude that Blanqui was willing to use the electoral campaign and the tribune of the Chamber of

---

13 See pp. 85-88 above.
14 Blanqui, *La Patrie en danger,* p. 278.
15 Blanqui, *Critique sociale,* I, 207-8.
16 Blanqui, *La Patrie en danger,* p. 274.
17 Blanqui, *Critique sociale,* I, 207.

Deputies as techniques of mass indoctrination under certain circumstances, but he was ever suspicious of the appeal that political office had for radical politicians and mistrustful of the political intelligence of the peasant majority.

The fact that Blanqui partially accepted the revolutionary potential of legal electioneering does not answer those criticisms directed against his lack of interest in the everyday economic aspirations of the proletariat. André Marty qualified his praise of Blanqui to observe: "The basic error of Blanqui and of the Blanquists was . . . their scorn for the defense of the immediate demands of the workers." [18]

Blanqui hesitated to commit his organization to the struggle for the daily wants of the proletariat, fearing that too great an interest in wages and hours would dull the political consciousness of the workers.[19] He did, however, look with considerable favor upon strikes over economic issues, although he believed that all wage increases gained from strikes were canceled out in the long run by price rises.[20] In these strikes he saw a means of limiting the cruel and arbitrary powers of the employers to break and degrade the workers; [21] he recognized that they were the most popular and natural vehicles of worker solidarity and felt that economic struggles which ended in strikes were "pregnant with civil war." [22] The strike was not an end in itself but a step in the direction of the proletarian conquest of political power.

Provisionally supported on the strike as a defense against capitalist oppression, the masses ought to concentrate all of their efforts toward political changes acknowledged as the only ones

[18] Marty, *Quelques Aspects de l'activité de Blanqui,* p. 20.
[19] Blanqui MSS, 9581, p. 49.
[20] Blanqui, *Critique sociale,* II, 20.
[21] *Ibid.,* p. 227.   [22] *Ibid.*

capable of implementing a social transformation and the just distribution of goods.[23]

Apparently the only practical manifestations of Blanqui's sympathy with strikes were the polemics he occasionally published against laws which restricted the rights of worker organizations.[24] During the 1860s, when many leaders of the French section of the First International were drifting into political action through their initial commitment to labor organization and agitation,[25] the Blanquists continued to conspire among the workers but without much interest in the powerful contemporary proletarian movement towards economic goals.

While he seemed to underestimate the political significance of economic agitation, Blanqui did realize that some sort of intellectual preparation was necessary to orient the masses toward revolutionary solutions of their problems. One would expect this to follow from his rather hazy understanding of the economic relationships between the worker and the capitalist economy and from his philosophic acceptance of the vital historical role of the idea. He was therefore much more sensitive to the importance of a prerevolutionary "enlightenment" of the masses, than to economic drives which might ultimately be focused upon political class conflict.

[23] *Ibid.*, p. 167. The idea of the strike as a political weapon combined with Blanqui's mistrust of parliamentary institutions, and his stress upon direct action may have had an indirect influence upon the revolutionary branch of French syndicalism. Sorel and the philosophers of this movement, however, represent the absolute intellectual antithesis of Blanqui's austere, though often shallow, rationalism.

[24] *Ibid.*, pp. 174-77; also Blanqui MSS, 9581, p. 112.

[25] A. Thomas, *Le Second Empire*, Vol. X of *Histoire Socialiste*, ed. J. Jaurès (Paris: Publications Jules Rouff et Cie., 1906), pp. 369-77.

Blanqui assumed that capitalist society was organized to blind the people to the real nature and cause of their unhappy condition. The enlightenment denied them by the possessing classes had to be supplied by the radical elite. During periods of political censorship, the same secrecy and determination required to prepare an insurrection had to be dedicated to the spread of ideas which could rally the proletariat against its enemies. Throughout his political life Blanqui labored to spread the revolutionary consciousness which he saw as the objective condition for the success of his projected insurrections.

In one of his early political pamphlets entitled *Propagande démocratique* the young agitator outlined the catastrophic effects for the republican cause of allowing the government to stifle all expression of dissent. All good republicans were obliged to combat antidemocratic prejudices and calumny by spreading the principles of equality and fraternity which would, in the end, set the masses in motion. Consequently Blanqui and his companion proposed to reprint and distribute excerpts from various republican writings which had been suppressed by the government.[26]

Twenty-five years after he had projected his "democratic propaganda" Blanqui confessed in a letter to a friend that he had been mistaken in his overemphasis on organization at the cost of mass agitation; "before organizing men one must draw them out of their lethargy." [27] He had come to believe that a revolution could only be made if an "electric current of ideas" activated the people,[28] who needed some outer impulsion before they would move. However, ideas

[26] Blanqui et Hadot-Desages, *Propagande démocratique,* pp. 1-2.
[27] Blanqui MSS, 9584 (part 1), pp. 117-18 (dated 1860).
[28] *Ibid.*

of any value could not be legally transmitted to the people
under an authoritarian regime, so clandestine propaganda
became the condition for the very existence of socialist organizations which could not even get recruits if there were
not some enthusiasm for socialism and equality among the
masses.[29]

The inculcation of the masses with a revolutionary spirit
was inseparably bound in Blanqui's mind with the spread
of atheism.[30]   When the opportunity presented itself, he
did try to carry out revolutionary propaganda through
short-lived anticlerical journals; thus the Blanquist sheet
Candide, published briefly in 1863, was dedicated to a
philosophic attack upon reactionary—that is, primarily religious—ideas.

The alert censors and gendarmes of a series of somewhat
less than democratic regimes quite often restricted Blanqui's opportunities for clandestine propaganda to the
spoken word. He managed personally to influence a remarkable number of fellow prisoners throughout his long
career.   Each imprisonment would send a new crop of
young Blanquists out into the Paris cafés which were the
great forum of subversive ideas during the century.[31]
These young men were usually students or intellectuals,
but many workers who had run afoul of the political police
were also indoctrinated by the self-styled proletarian revolutionary.

One other channel for the oral propagation of seditious

29 *Ibid.,* pp. 119-21.
30 *Ibid.,* 9590 (part 2), p. 356. "[The people] will become seriously
revolutionary only through atheism."
31 Paul Lafargue wrote: "A. Blanqui holds the honor of having
given a revolutionary education to a section of the youth of our
generation." *La Révolution Française,* April 20, 1879. Cf. Clemenceau's
description in *Le Journal,* Nov. 27, 1896.

doctrines was the use of public trials as a political forum. Blanqui was very conscious of the potentialities of this technique. When, for example, his disciple Tridon was indicted for conspiring against the Second Empire, the old professional advised the youth to plan calmly a vigorous and aggressive defense—a program which might call down reprisals but would serve, at the same time, to mobilize public opinion.[32]

Blanqui himself brought a lifetime of unrivaled experience to the perfection of the role of defendant at a political trial. He usually began by denying the competence of the court and accusing it of political or class bias; then he would verbally indict and convict the institutions of capitalist society and go on to outline some of his own prescriptions for social justice. He almost invariably received a harsh sentence, but had, at least, the satisfaction of reading his most inflammatory utterances in the official journals.

BLANQUI'S FRUITLESS CAUTION

Blanqui's recognition of the importance of agitation which might educate the masses in the long run should not obscure his obvious primary commitment to insurrection. His slogan under almost any circumstances remained: "Weapons and organization, these are the decisive elements of progress, the real means for ending misery." [33]   However it is worth noting that, in theory at least, the hardbitten conspirator did not find the solution of all social problems in the mere act of insurrection.

In the spirit of his century he rejected any simple mecha-

[32] In a letter to Tridon in Blanqui MSS, 9589, pp. 36-37.
[33] In his toast to the London exiles, *Avis au Peuple* (Feb. 10, 1851), reprinted in Dommanget, *Blanqui à Belle-Ile,* p. 66.

nistic or voluntarist view of social development and actually arrived at the position that catastrophic social changes were either destructive or superficial.[34] The characteristic social organism or an epoch could not simply be remade according to a priori ideas but was, like a current fed by a thousand sources, the product of its entire past.[35] As for revolutions:

Revolutions themselves, which appear to be so fortuitous, are actually the products of a long period of incubation.[36]

The longed-for Revolution was then the product of slowly maturing forces which no group of men could manufacture. As it happened, Blanqui was certain that France had long embodied all of the historical conditions of a revolutionary situation. Therefore, one might dismiss his intellectual qualifications of revolutionary action as of no practical significance. The record of his failures would certainly seem to indicate a persistent indifference to the objective revolutionary potentialities of his time. Paradoxically, this conclusion is contradicted by the details of his revolutionary career. In *every* political crisis after 1839 with which we connect Blanqui, we find that he actually attempted to postpone the violent consummation of the movements he had helped to organize because the immediate circumstances were not propitious for a revolution.

There is a suggestion of Blanqui's caution even in his preparations for the coup of May, 1839, but the outlines of his reluctant putschism are first seen clearly during the stirring revolutionary period of 1848.

When he was released from prison in February, 1848, he

34 Blanqui, *Critique sociale,* I, 41.
35 Blanqui MSS, 9591 (part 2), p. 520.
36 Blanqui, *Critique sociale,* I, 41.

was immediately accepted as the leader of the most radical
republican and socialist elements in Paris. On the evening
of February 25, the day after Blanqui's arrival in Paris,
the most militant leftists in the city, disgusted with Lamartine's successful defense of the tricolor against the red flag,
met to consider a coup against the Provisional Government. They awaited only the word of Blanqui, the martyred and implacable conspirator, to rush into the streets.
To the consternation of the militants and to the delighted
surprise of the agents of the police, Blanqui counseled caution. He spoke of the danger of frightening the *bourgeoisie* and the peasants by forcing into power men who
had reputations as extremists. "If we seize power by an
audacious *coup de main,* like robbers in the shadows of the
night," he asked, "who will answer for the duration of our
power?" [37]

Blanqui predicted that the feeble occupants of the Hôtel
de Ville (i.e., the Provisional Government) would inevitably fall, but only when the great masses of the *faubourgs*
decided to achieve a "new 10th of August." [38] Then
would the government be delivered into the hands of the
"truly popular" leaders of the revolutionary clubs. In
terms completely foreign to putschism Blanqui rejected
any socialist conquest of power which was not borne along
on the crest of a mass movement.

There is little doubt that Blanqui helped to organize
and lead mass demonstrations during the turbulent months

[37] Quoted by a hostile contemporary, A. Lucas, *Les clubs et les
clubistes* (Paris: E. Dentu, 1851), p. 214. Also described in Bernard,
Curiosités révolutionnaires (Paris: O. Giraud et J. Dagneau, Librairies-
Éditeurs, 1851), pp. 36-37.

[38] August 10, 1792—the revolutionary sections of Paris invaded the
Tuileries and overthrew the monarchy.

of March and April in order to exert a continuous pressure on the government from the left.[39]   On March 17 a vast crowd marched in a procession to the Hôtel de Ville to present petitions for the removal of regular troops from Paris and the postponement of the scheduled elections for the new National Assembly. Blanqui, as the leader of a political club, joined the deputation which presented the crowd's demands to the frightened members of the Provisional Government.

For all revolutionary purposes the "day" was a fiasco as Louis Blanc and Ledru-Rollin, fearing that men like Blanqui might gain control of the Paris masses, added their eloquence to Lamartine's and, without actually accepting the petitions, persuaded the people to disband peaceably.[40]

Many contemporary observers believed that Blanqui planned to overthrow the Provisional Government, or at least purge it of its moderate majority on March 17,[41] but he himself denied this. He admitted to having organized the demonstration but claimed that after the clubs refused to petition for an indefinite postponement of the elections,

[39] According to Blanqui, when a bourgeois politician asked him whether, "You wish to overthrow us," he responded, "No! But to bar the road behind you."   L. A. Blanqui, *Résponse du citoyen Auguste Blanqui* (Paris: Imprimerie D'Ad. Blondeau, 1848), p. 2.

[40] D. Stern (Mme D'Agoult), *Histoire de la Révolution de 1848* (Paris: Calmann Lévy, 1878), II, 193-201.

[41] Cf. E. Regnault, *Histoire du gouvernement provisoire* (Paris: Victor Lecou, 1850), p. 224; Garnier-Pagès, *Histoire de la Révolution de 1848* (Paris: Pagnerre, 1861), VI, 430.   Daniel Stern describes Blanqui's position at the meeting of the clubs, before the procession, as follows: "Blanqui himself . . . did not dare say that it was necessary to overthrow the Provisional Government, and spoke only of purging it." Stern, *Histoire de la Révolution*, II, 193. For a sympathizer who thought that Blanqui intended a purge of the moderate members of the government, see G. Lefrançais, *Souvenirs d'un révolutionnaire* (Bruxelles: Imprimerie Ch. Hautstont, 1902), p. 32.

he followed along to the Hôtel de Ville but "with complete indifference." [42]

Wasserman's careful conclusion that there is no proof at all that Blanqui planned a violent coup [43] seems to be the most that one can safely assume from the evidence. If he did have putsch in mind he certainly did virtually nothing to implement it.

Again on April 16, a demonstration of the discontented Paris workers was planned. This time the government lined the streets with the armed National Guard so that the crowd was forced to satisfy itself with a rather abject parade between rows of bourgeois bayonets.[44] Once again the question arises as to whether Blanqui intended to use the movement as a springboard for a *coup de main*.[45] Wasserman deduced that, by this time, the implacable hostility of the government must have impelled Blanqui to abandon hope of influencing events by any method other than the application of force.[46] Many of Blanqui's contemporaries felt certain that the fearsome *conspirateur monomane* [47] did, in fact, commit himself to an insurrec-

[42] *Le Moniteur Universel,* March 15, 1849 (Blanqui's testimony before the Haute Cour de Justice, Audience of March 13), also *ibid.,* April 3, 1849 (his testimony on March 31).

[43] Wasserman, *Les Clubs de Barbès et de Blanqui,* p. 73.

[44] A. R. Calman, *Ledru-Rollin and the Second French Republic* (New York: Columbia University Press, 1922), pp. 150-60.

[45] Blanqui had a private interview with Lamartine several days before the demonstration and apparently also tried to see Ledru-Rollin. There is no evidence, however, that he plotted with any of the members of the government. There is a highly colored and improbable account of his talk with Lamartine in: A. Lamartine, *Histoire de la Révolution de 1848* (Leipzig: Brockhaus & Avenarius, 1849), I, 160-65. On the attempted meeting with Ledru-Rollin, see Caussidière, *Mémoires* (3rd ed.; Paris: Michel Lévy Frères, 1849), II, 14.

[46] Wasserman, *Les Clubs de Barbès et de Blanqui,* p. 122.

[47] Blanqui is so described by Lamartine in the latter's deposition

tion on April 16.[48]   The conspirator himself denied any
conspiratorial intent, claiming that he appeared at the
Champ de Mars, the field where the demonstrations had
assembled, only to distribute copies of his response to the
accusations of his political enemies.[49]   As in the case of
March 17, one cannot say for certain that Blanqui had not
prepared a coup for April 16, but again there is almost no
direct evidence that he did.

After the very disappointing spring of the February
Revolution, Blanqui apparently finally decided that it was
necessary to return to conspiracy.   The reason he had not
done this before, he explained to his club after the April
16 fiasco, was that such techniques:

recall only too well the tyrannical past—that he hoped to eschew
this alternative under a democratic regime, but, as the counter-
revolution had been organized, he proposed to name section
chiefs and to organize the central republican society on the basis
of the old secret societies.[50]

It is quite possible that Blanqui's club began to organize

for the Commission D'Enquête, *Pièces relatives aux événements du 15
Mai et l'insurrection de Juin* (Bordeaux: Imprimerie de Durand), p.
168.

[48] Garnier-Pagès, *Histoire de la Révolution de 1848,* VII, 369-71:
Stern, *Histoire de la Révolution de 1848,* II, 297.   Carlier, chief of the
police assigned to the Ministry of the Interior, testified that Blanqui
planned the assassination of some members of the government.   Commission D'Enquête, *Pièces relatives aux événements du 15 Mai,* p. 112.

[49] *Le Moniteur Universel,* March 21, 1849 (Blanqui's testimony before the Haute Cour de Justice, Audience of March 19).   For observers
convinced that Blanqui had planned no insurrection for April 16 see
L. Blanc, *Histoire de la Révolution de 1848* (Paris: Libraire Internationale, 1870), II, 14-16; Proudhon, *Confessions d'un révolutionnaire,* p. 94.   Proudhon felt that the rank and file probably pushed
the movements of April 16 and March 17 further than Blanqui and
the other radical leaders had intended.   "In revolution, the leaders
propose and the people dispose."

[50] Quoted in *La Commune de Paris,* April 19, 1848.

a conspiratorial movement in a secret session on April 17.[51]
Therefore a revolutionary *apparat* may well have been in
existence during the next great political crisis on May 15.
If so, it could have had little effect on the chaotic events
of this "day." A mob which gathered to demand the liberation of Poland broke into the National Assembly and,
after several hours of inconsequential shouting, declared
the Assembly to be dissolved, rushed to the Hôtel de Ville,
and promulgated a revolutionary government which was
very shortly liquidated by the loyal troops of the National
Guard.[52] Blanqui's role in these events seem to have been
first, one of reluctant participation, and then, disgusted
rejection of the entire affair.

Although he accompanied the crowd when it invaded
the Hôtel de Ville he had no enthusiasm for its avowed
purpose, which was to force the Assembly to take some
concrete action for Polish independence. He spoke from
the rostrum in an apparent effort to turn the minds of the
mob from the question of Poland to French social and economic injustice [53] but when other orators persuaded the
frenzied people to seize the Hôtel de Ville and form a revolutionary government, Blanqui remained behind, sadly
aware that the chaotic onslaught would fail.[54]

He was tried in 1849 for his part in this coup, and in his
defense he denied both responsibility for, and sympathy
with, the entire affair.[55] Not only did he insist that he

[51] This was attested at Blanqui's trial in 1849 by a certain Altraff
and not denied by the defendant. *Compte rendu de l'affaire du 15
Mai*, pp. 110-11 (Audience of March 13, before the Haute Cour de
Justice).

[52] Stern, *Histoire de la Révolution*, III, 24-51.

[53] *Le Moniteur Universel*, May 17, 1848.

[54] *Ibid.*, March 15, 1849. (Blanqui's testimony before the Haut
Cour de Justice, Audience of March 13).

[55] The summary of the evidence for the prosecution's contention

would have accepted the authority of any National Assembly elected by universal suffrage, but he admitted that there was no real support in Paris or in the country at large for a new revolutionary government, which would have been overthrown in a few days by the frightened and unsophisticated peasantry.

The defendant pointed out that he had definitely spoken against the projected May 15 demonstration at his club. Indeed, if he had really wanted to dissolve the National Assembly he would not have wasted time in speeches, nor waited to seize the Hôtel de Ville until the bourgeois National Guard had assembled and the crowd begun to disperse. Moreover it was ridiculous to assume that he could have impressed his will upon the crowd in that situation. The opinion that one leads the masses is comical. On the contrary one is sometimes led by the masses where one does not wish to go.

Why then had he followed the crowd if he disapproved of its actions? Blanqui reasoned:

Was it necessary to sacrifice popularity to prudence? Puritans can make a great deal of this and moralize endlessly about it. As for me, I believed that I had a mission to fulfill and I did not intend to disregard it. I said, "You wish to go to the demonstration? Let us go then but watch out for stupid blunders." [56]

However, when the crowd was finally persuaded by the foolish eloquence of Barbès and Huber to march on the Hôtel de Ville, Blanqui felt that he could be of no more

that Blanqui did plot an insurrection on May 15, is in *Le Moniteur Universel,* March 28, 1849.

[56] There is a draft of this speech in the Blanqui MSS, 9590 (part 2), pp. 386-406; also in *Le Moniteur Universel,* April 3, 1849.

The minutes of the trial have been abridged in several publications, e.g., E. Duquai, *Les Grands procès politiques—les accusés du 15 Mai 1848* (Paris: Armand Le Chevalier, 1869); *Compte Rendu de l'affaire du 15 Mai.*

use to the benighted people and sadly watched the debacle from the sidelines.

There is more than enough evidence to verify Blanqui's description of his conduct during the May crisis.[57]   On the other hand, it may be argued that Blanqui, if cautious on May 15, was in general working toward an illegal assault on the new Republic and the appeals to violence heard at his club throughout April and May contributed to the atmosphere which made a rising inevitable.[58]   From a purely activist point of view, however, Blanqui's practical revolutionary contributions are summed up in Suzanne Wasserman's rather bitter estimate of his behavior on May 15: "As on the 25th of February, as on the 17th of March, as on the 16th of April, when the moment came to act, Blanqui backed out, not finding the occasion propitious." [59]

The culmination of the class and political struggle in June of 1848 found Blanqui already in prison.   From late May, 1849, until 1859, he was forced to satisfy himself with the role of observer and critic.

The letters which Blanqui wrote from his prisons at Doullens and Belle-Ile contain several significant passages on the possibilities for revolutionary agitation during the period.   By the fall of 1848 he was cautioning the workers of Paris that any sort of physical conflict would be useless under the existing circumstances.[60]   In 1853, he wrote that the widespread commercial prosperity under the Bonapartist regime rendered the hopes for the success or even the

[57] Considerable testimony to this effect, given before the Haute Cour de Justice in 1849, can be found in *Le Moniteur Universel,* March 24, 1849.   Cf. Stern, *Histoire de la Révolution de 1848,* III, 24; *Le Représentant du peuple,* May 15, 1848.

[58] Wasserman, *Les Clubs de Barbès et de Blanqui,* pp. 164-65.

[59] *Ibid.,* p. 181.

[60] Blanqui MSS, 9581, pp. 143-45, "Réponse à la demande d'un toast pour le Banquet des Travailleurs," (Nov., 1848).

growth of a revolutionary party illusory.[61]   In 1860, he again found conditions unpropitious for an insurrection, but encouraged his friends to begin the work for a revolution by stimulating the masses through the spread of socialist ideas.[62]

These scattered statements by no means exemplify a rejection of a belief in the supreme desirability of a revolution.   They do indicate that Blanqui recognized certain conditions as the prerequisites of a successful insurrection and that he did not always find the required conditions when he examined contemporary society.   One might add that Blanqui seemed somewhat more pessimistic about the objective chances for a revolution when he himself was in prison—his periods of freedom during the 1860s were passed, as usual, in organizing the disciplined conspiracy which was to be the shock battalion of the imminent class war.[63]   He was released from prison in 1860 and arrested again in 1861 for conspiracy to overthrow the government. He escaped in 1865 and directed a new Parisian conspiracy from his refuge in Belgium.

Blanqui managed to fashion a secret organization which, at its peak, mustered approximately two thousand students and workers dedicated to a conquest of political power at the first favorable opportunity.[64]   The question of opportunity arose during the summer of 1870 when news of French defeats made Paris a frightened and restless city in which the overt hostility to the Second Empire grew bolder and more popular each day.[65]   Blanqui's young lieutenants

[61] *Ibid.*, 9584 (part 1), p. 86.   [62] *Ibid.*, pp. 117-18.

[63] *La Gazette des Tribunaux*, June 16, 1861. Da Costa, *Les Blanquistes*, pp. 14-31.

[64] *Ibid.*, p. 31.

[65] J. Tchernoff, *Le Parti républicain au coup d'état et sous le Second Empire* (Paris: A. Pedone, 1906), p. 598.

excitedly urged that their organization take advantage of the popular discontent and begin an immediate insurrection against the imperial government. They pointed out that the conspiracy had already lost a majority of its adherents through its inaction and that a further postponement of the coup which was its *raison d'être* would alienate the enthusiasts who remained.

In a council of war held on August 13, 1870, Blanqui argued the imprudence of an insurrection under existing circumstances and went so far as to suggest to a wildly militant disciple that his urge to commit suicide could just as easily be fulfilled by leaping out of a third story window.[66] Finally, however, the commander in chief acceded to the wishes of his troops. On August 14 he led a handful of the faithful in an *attentat* which received absolutely no support from the Parisian workers (who were to overthrow the Empire within three weeks), and petered out in the middle of an empty street before government forces had even arrived on the scene.[67]

On September 4 the revolution which the Blanquists had prematurely invoked was consummated. A strong case can be made for the very important contributions of the Blanquist organization to the successful overthrow of the Second Empire.[68] Although they shared the leadership of this revolt, they were not able to share its fruits with the leaders of the liberal *bourgeoisie*.

The last revolutionary action of Blanqui's career oc-

[66] Da Costa, *Les Blanquistes,* pp. 32-33; Dommanget, *Blanqui, la guerre de 1870-71 et la Commune,* p. 12.

[67] This affair has been described by Blanqui himself in *La Patrie en danger,* pp. 49-61.

[68] Dommanget, *Blanqui, la guerre de 1870-71 et la Commune,* pp. 21-27. Here, considerable evidence of Blanquist planning and participation on September 4 is presented.

curred on October 31, 1870, when a great crowd of Parisians invaded the Hôtel de Ville and attempted to install a
new government of various radical leaders. Blanqui, who
at first had rallied to the government of National Defense,
repudiated the *union sacrée* when he concluded that the
bourgeois politicians were treasonably halfhearted in their
defense of Paris against the Prussians.[69]   In late October he
wrote a series of inflammatory articles in his paper, *La
Patrie en danger,* which certainly could be interpreted as
incitements to insurrection,[70] but apparently he did not
envisage or support the immediate application of his political slogans on October 31.[71]

When he learned that he had been named as a member
of the revolutionary government he went to the Hôtel de
Ville and did his best to organize some sort of revolutionary
power.   The leaders of the Government of National Defense, however, managed to rally enough loyal troops to
drive out the radicals and their partisans in the National
Guard, so that once more a movement of which Blanqui
had not originally approved, but in which he dutifully
participated, was defeated.[72]

We have then the characteristic development of Blanqui's
reluctant voluntarism: first, his arrival in Paris marked by
the scars of his most recent imprisonment and the aura of
revolutionary prestige; then, his organization of young

[69] Blanqui, *La Patrie en danger,* pp. 68-71.

[70] Dommanget, *Blanqui, la guerre de 1870-71 et la Commune,* pp. 76-84.

[71] Lefrançais recalls a conversation with Blanqui on the morning of October 31: "Blanqui also realized that it was necessary to oppose the Hôtel de Ville [i.e., the government] and to put an end to its proj- ects.   But he is not for overthrowing the government."   Lefrançais, *Souvenirs d'un révolutionnaire,* p. 415.

[72] Dommanget, *Blanqui, la guerre de 1870-71 et la Commune,* pp. 76-84.

students and workers into clubs or supposedly disciplined conspiratorial groups, his vigorous and able attacks on the *status quo* in the press and from the tribune, his recognition that the objective conditions for a proletarian revolution were not present, his capitulation to a spontaneous movement of the masses or to the insistence of his presumed subordinates that an insurrection be attempted; and the characteristic denouement in which, as Geffroy observed, "the chief followed the soldiers" [73] to political disaster.

[73] Geffroy, *L'Enfermé*, II, 59.

CHAPTER EIGHT

The Theory of Permanent Insurrection

THE FACT THAT Blanqui, the professional of conspiracy and revolutionary discipline par excellence, should have been led time and again into adventures which he theoretically condemned illuminates certain interesting aspects of his career, his ideas, and of the nature of conspiratorial politics.

Geffroy has observed that Blanqui, although essentially a "man of thought," was widely known as the "living symbol of revolutionary action" because his ideas led him into continuous physical conflict with his society. In time, Geffroy conjectures, Blanqui's real personality was changed by its social image and "he was sometimes constrained to obey his legend." [1]

It was probably Blanqui's famous revolutionary integrity, his absolute commitment to the cause at any price, rather than any ideas he voiced, which attracted so many young militants to his side. Perhaps this was the reason for the great blow to his prestige in March of 1848 when the "Taschereau Document," purporting to establish his previous complicity with the police, was published.[2] For Blanqui ever to have cooperated with the reactionary police under any circumstances was the very negation of his political being. Even an unproved allegation did him considerable damage.

Blanqui was bound for life to his manifest role as the Galahad of revolution *à outrance*. This forced him some-

1 Geffroy, *L'Enfermé*, II, 39-41.
2 See pp. 9-10 above.

times to act in ways which he himself realized were not suited to his immediate political goals. A prisoner of his own reputation, he reluctantly followed his disciples into "Blanquist" adventures which Blanqui the theorist had forsworn.

Another reason for the misfortunes of Blanquism, at least during those periods when the radical movement was forced underground, lay in the nature of the Carbonarist type of revolutionary organization to which Blanqui character- istically adhered. Ideally, the organizations were estab- lished along the following lines: At the bottom of the revolutionary pyramid were the small cells of the rank and file, completely isolated from one another and from all their leaders except the agent who had organized them. Each organizer was in contact with only one superior in the con- spiracy but might be responsible for several subsidiary units. This structure was followed from echelon to echelon upward to the leaders who controlled all of the elements of the conspiracy and were themselves known to but a few trusted lieutenants.[3]

Actual conditions qualified this intensive secrecy in several ways. It can be assumed that if potential recruits had not had some idea of the leaders of the conspiracy they would not have joined it. Secondly, the homogeneity, both in previous political experience and social background of the groups which furnished most of the conspirators, must

[3] For a description of the Blanquist organization in the 1830s, L. De la Hodde, *Histoire des sociétés secrètes et du parti républicain* (Paris: Julien, Lanier et Cie., 1850), pp. 199-203. This work, by a former police spy, is very questionable in parts, but apparently accurate on the structure of the Blanquist conspiracy. Cf. Zévaès, *Une Révolution manquée*, p. 47. For the organization in the 1860s, Da Costa, *Les Blanquistes*, p. 26; Dommanget, "Les Groupes Blanquistes de la fin du Second Empire," *Revue Socialiste*, XLIV (Feb., 1951), 225-31.

have led to some recognition of mutual participation beyond the borders of the supposedly isolated cells. When the Blanquists appeared in secret formation at the funeral of Victor Noir, Jules Vallès, who was active on the periphery of the movement, immediately recognized and identified most of them.[4]

Then, there were occasions when the pressure of events led the Blanquists to suspend some of their precautions and meet in relatively large groups. We find a group of Blanquists meeting at a Paris *café* in 1866, in order to censure and expel some members who had disobeyed their chief by attending meetings of the First International at Geneva. The meeting was surprised by the police and forty-one Blanquists were arrested.[5]

It is evident, however, that a fairly high standard of secrecy was usually maintained since Blanqui was sometimes able to plan and begin insurrections without having them anticipated and forestalled by the police. Indeed it was only with the utmost precautions that anyone could have sustained a secret organization under the noses of the celebrated French police spies and *agents provocateurs*. The longer such secrecy had to be sustained, the greater were the chances of betrayal and the stronger the pressure for immediate action.

This pressure was intensified by the nature of the goals and structure of a Blanquist conspiracy. The goal was a *coup de force* in the immediate future. The knowledge of this object and the penalties which failure would entail, when combined with a discipline of deepest secrecy, must

---

[4] J. Vallès, *L'Insurgé* (Paris: Bibliothèque-Charpentier, 1914), pp. 150-59.

[5] Da Costa, *Les Blanquistes*, p. 20.

have engendered considerable tension among the rank and file. The young idealists were staking their lives on a violent assault upon the powers of their society; under nameless leaders with unknown forces and tactics at their disposal; at a moment selected by them which might be tomorrow, next week, or perhaps, the followers began to suspect, never. One would expect to find an urge to get the thing over with and a pressure on the leadership from below to end the period of almost unbearable expectation. The formation of an elite dedicated to unquestioning but undefined action engendered the necessity to make use of the revolutionary enthusiasm before it could be dissipated by discouragement and scepticism. In referring to 1839 when, presumably, Blanqui was not pushed into insurrection but rationally chose his moment, Louis Blanc was impelled to the observation that:

The conspirators were seized with a fatal restlessness and impatience; they longed to fight, and declared that they would separate if the word were not given them to take up arms—the members of the committee felt themselves fatally entangled by circumstances. Their army was lost to them if it did not hurry them along with it, and an iron hand drove them down a declivity, up which there is no returning after a first rash step.[6]

This urge to relieve the tension of secrecy and danger by immediate action might be considered in relation to George Simmel's notion of "the temptation of betrayal." According to Simmel's analysis, the possessor of a secret needs to

[6] Blanc, *The History of Ten Years,* II, 606. Cf. De la Hodde, *Histoire des sociétés secrètes,* p. 231. "The Committee directing the Society of Seasons in 1839 knew that the pressure was going to become intense and that a positive promise of action was necessary to satisfy impatience." De la Hodde notes the same circumstance in the conspiracy of the republican Society of the Rights of Man in 1833, when "The tail led the head, as was customary," *ibid.,* p. 121.

share it to render it meaningful.[7] Only by passing from secret to open warfare against the government could the Blanquist justify his previous submission to the rules of silence and obedience. The desire to justify secrecy by action might, if frustrated, lead to the immediate justification through incautious revelations to family and friends.

These partial explanations for the long tale of Blanquist misfortune do not completely answer the question: Why did Blanqui persist in this particular ill-advised form of revolutionary endeavor? The observation that oppressive governments force any sincere opposition into illegal conspiracy provides no answer because there are many alternatives of clandestine organization and underground political tactics beside the techniques to which Blanqui usually adhered. Perhaps the question can be answered by reference to Blanqui's personality, or his social class,[8] or his historical relation to a particular French political tradition.[9] None of these answers, however, gives us Blanqui's own reasons

[7] George Simmel, "The Sociology of Secrecy and Secret Societies," *American Journal of Sociology*, XI (June, 1906), 465-66.

[8] Blanquist theory is often labeled *petit bourgeois*. The evidence for this characterization is to be sought not in Blanqui's class background, nor even in the class composition of his following, but in the degree to which his ideology and actions reflect the aspirations and the historical situation of the lower-middle class. His economic theory, based upon a hatred of usury, would seem to fit this description, but his statist collectivism and rejection of piecemeal property redistributions hardly belong to it. Whether Blanquism was essentially "*petit bourgeois*" is an unresolvable, and perhaps meaningless, question.

[9] See p. 121 above. Sombart believed that the lower-middle-class orientation of French radicalism and the attributes of French national character evolved a socialist movement characteristically devoted to "Factionism, Clubism, and Putschism." W. Sombart, *Socialism and the Social Movement*, tr. M. Epstein (New York: E. P. Dutton and Co., 1919), pp. 156-65.

for his actions or the relationship between his political tactics and his own ideas.

BLANQUIST TACTICS AND THE IDEA OF REVOLUTION

This relationship can be illuminated by reexamining the practical significance of the influence of philosophic idealism upon Blanqui's social philosophy.[10] His interpretation of the historical role of the Idea leads, him, perforce, to an acceptance of the revolutionary role of a conspiracy of the elite.

Given his assumption that an unenlightened people can never be truly revolutionary, Blanqui faced the problem of achieving that popular revolution which he believed to be the precondition of mass enlightenment. Under an aristocratic or bourgeois regime the means of popular instruction must obviously be denied the people who, therefore, lack the knowledge which would impel them to revolt. But only a revolution can enlighten them. How could this dilemma be resolved? [11]

The only answer lay in the existence of a small group whose knowledge of the roots of oppression was not coupled with the desire to profit by it. Since the great mass was too ignorant to free itself, the instructed and altruistic few would have to strike the first blows in the battle for the freedom of all. This revolutionary elite would have to make up what it lacked in numbers by determination, organization, and a shrewd reading of the historical condi-

[10] Cf. Mason, "Blanqui and Communism," *Political Science Quarterly*, XLIV (Dec., 1929), 505. "It is essential to know something of Blanqui's views on the importance of education and the role of the idea in history in order to understand his justification of his revolutionary method."

[11] See pp. 55-56 above.

tions necessary for revolutionary enterprise. Its ability to elicit mass support before the revolution would be limited by the legal and political structure it was committed to overthrow. Therefore, its eventual purpose of instructing the masses could only be effected by cutting itself off from them in order safely to fashion a clandestine force which could strike off the chains forged by capitalism and its allies.

This elite could only be recruited from the *déclassés* of modern urban society. Notwithstanding Blanqui's harsh strictures against the middle-class leaders of the radical parties, he flatly rejected the idea of excluding the *bourgeoisie* from proletarian organizations. In words similar to Lenin's he affirmed the vital role of the bourgeois revolutionary in enlightening and leavening the masses.[12] It was the *bourgeoisie* which had first inscribed the doctrine of equality upon the banner of the proletariat, and "everywhere there are the bourgeois who lead the people in its battles against the *bourgeoisie*."[13] The fact that the proletariat finds bourgeois allies and leaders in no way contradicts the fact that the basic conflict is between "the *bourgeoisie* and the people, between profit and wages, between capital and labor."[14] The tendency to restrict membership in unions and in proletarian organizations, such as the First International, to workers was in Blanqui's

[12] Cf. V. I. Lenin, "What Is to Be Done?" *Marx—Engels—Marxism* (Moscow: Foreign Languages Publishing House, 1947), p. 126.

[13] Quoted in Dommanget, *Blanqui à Belle-Ile,* p. 76. There is a rather amusing piece in a workers' journal in 1879 which decides the question of whether Blanqui, born into the middle class, can be considered a true proletarian, in the affirmative. *Le Prolétaire,* Aug. 23, 1879.

[14] Blanqui MSS, 9581, p. 151.

eyes a disguised maneuver of the reactionaries—an attempt to reestablish the feudal corporations and the *compagnonnage* of the *ancien régime*.[15]

It is partly true, as E. S. Mason remarks, that Blanqui expected the leadership of the proletarian revolution to rest in the hands of the *bourgeoisie*.[16] However, Blanqui's reliance upon the revolutionary role of the bourgeois *déclassé* can be overstated. It should be observed that he used the word *déclassé* in two senses—to refer to the declassed bourgeois intellectual but also to refer to the workers who had been declassed by a relatively high degree of enlightenment. This is clearly illustrated by Blanqui's critique of proposals to establish *écoles professionelles* for intelligent workers. These propositions he interpreted as efforts to construct a "caste system" which allowed the natural leaders of the people to be siphoned off into the ruling class. "Ability without money is only a danger for tyranny," he observed. To assure an intelligent worker of a high income was a clever way to remove him from the ranks of the *déclassés* who are the "secret leaven of the masses." [17] Thus the enlightened Paris worker, filled with intelligence and understanding,[18] not only constituted the revolutionary rank and file, but contributed a significant element to the cadre of the prerevolutionary elite.

The Blanquist leaders, like their master, were primarily,

---

[15] Blanqui, *Critique sociale,* II, 348 (dated 1868).

[16] Mason, "Blanqui and Communism," *Political Science Quarterly,* XLIV (Dec., 1929), 507. Mason quotes Blanqui's strongest statement to this effect: "The *bourgeoisie* includes an elite minority, an indissoluble group, nervous, ardent and full of zeal; it is the essence, the soul, the life, of the Revolution."

[17] Blanqui, *Critique sociale,* I, 218-20. Naturally he was always suspicious of those who feared universal education would lead to the *déclassement* of the workers. Blanqui MSS, 9590 (part 1), pp. 381-82.

[18] *Ni Dieu Ni Maître,* Dec. 3, 1880.

although not exclusively, recruited from the ranks of the middle class. It is, however, probably incorrect to observe with Mason and others that "the Blanquist party itself was composed principally of members of the bourgeoisie, radical students of the schools of Paris, young advocates, and journalists." [19] Although evidence of this nature cannot be absolutely validated, contemporary descriptions of the Blanquists during the three periods (1836-39; 1848; and the 1860s) when they actually constituted a formal organization seem to indicate that Blanqui's following contained more proletarians than any group but the Proudhonists, and that the majority of his organization was drawn from the working class.[20]

The great reservoir of Blanqui's revolutionary elite, whether proletarian or bourgeois *déclassé*, was Paris. There would be found the cadre for the insurrection, and there only the mass support for the successful consummation of a revolution. This support would come from the Paris workingmen whose unparalleled intelligence constituted their "principal strength." [21] The Parisian worker, spiritually and intellectually the antithesis of a brutalized peasantry, was free of that Catholic fetishism which had blinded the rural masses to their true interests.[22] These interests were shared by the people of Paris *and* understood by them.

Here Blanqui's conception of the relations between the

[19] Mason, "Blanqui and Communism," *Political Science Quarterly*, XLIV (Dec., 1929), 508.

[20] De la Hodde, *Histoire des sociétés secrètes*, p. 217; Wasserman, *Les Clubs de Barbès et de Blanqui*, p. 16; Dommanget, "Les Groupes Blanquistes de la fin du Second Empire," *Revue Socialiste* XLIV (Feb., 1951), 227-28.

[21] Blanqui, "Instructions pour une prise d'armes," *Archiv fur die Geschichte des Arbeiterbewegung*, XV (1930), 293.

[22] *Ni Dieu Ni Maître*, Dec. 11, 1880.

class struggle and revolutionary politics is worked out with a heavy emphasis upon voluntarist and intellectual factors and virtually no reference to the long-run political potential of the industrial proletariat viewed as a specific socio-economic group. Blanqui's Parisian workers are virtually indistinguishable from "the people" of Jacobin mythology— "this Parisian folk, the precursors of the future, the leaders of humanity, this prophetic and martyred people." [23] Sociologically, the proletarian elements of "this Parisian folk" were not, in the nineteenth century, equivalent to the factory proletariat of an industrial center such as Lyons. The typical occupation of the Blanquist workers captured in 1866 were cabinetmaker, carpenter, silversmith, etc.[24] Although Blanqui saw political promise in the early struggles of the Lyons proletariat, his conception of a revolutionary elite was always focused on the Paris of artisans and intellectuals.

It may be argued that Blanqui's conception of the peculiar political role of Paris was valid when it was formulated. The political and intellectual leadership of France was, and remains to this day, centered in its capital. The revolutionary movements of the nineteenth century flowered in the streets of Paris and there the political fate of the nation was often decided. As Blanqui observed, the arbitrary acts of Paris had put France on the path of progress in 1789, 1830, and 1848.[25]

A defense of Blanquist tactics based upon these considerations is usually qualified by the admission that the tactics became increasingly obsolete after 1850.[26] The reason that

[23] Blanqui MSS, 9581, p. 5. See p. 96 above.
[24] Da Costa, *Les Blanquistes*, pp. 21-22.
[25] Blanqui MSS, 9581, p. 145.
[26] E.g., A. Thomas, *Le Second Empire*, p. 332.

he clung to them almost until the end lies not merely in too sanguine an assessment of nineteenth-century social and political realities but in the retention of an eighteenth-century political mystique. This was the belief that Paris embodied the "general will" of the French nation.

Paris was the mind of France [27]—it had assumed the ancient duty of the French crown to protect the peasantry —but, most important, it was the *véritable représentation nationale*.[28] This was the case even when the rest of the nation freely repudiated the will of Paris in its election of a national legislature, for:

Paris, the true representative, the concentrated essence of the nation, dominates the assembly [i.e., the legislature] which is only its material and nominal emanation.[29]

Paris would only cease to represent the nation if it were occupied by an enemy, or on that day when the entire country had accepted the Parisian principle of equality. Until that time even a Parisian dictatorship could legitimately be described as "the government of the country by the country." [30]

The Revolution, then, must be made by the enlightened few; it must be consummated in the streets of Paris; and, under most regimes, it must be prepared in secret. Insurrectionist tactics might certainly be derived from all of this but are not necessarily implied. A disciplined revolutionary group might work for years in a clandestine manner to enlighten the workers, infiltrate and control their organizations, and lead them in their daily economic struggles, without ever committing itself to insurrectionist practices. Blanqui, however, as late as 1871, persisted in his attempt

---

27 Blanqui MSS, 9581, p. 32.
28 *Ibid.*, p. 121.   29 *Ibid.*, p. 93.
30 Blanqui, *Critique sociale*, I, 208.

to *begin* the proletarian revolution by leading a handful of militants to conquer state power. Why this was so can be partially descried in his interpretation of the history of revolutions.

Blanqui defined "revolution," in France at least, as a continuous process. The struggle which began in 1789 had never ended; it repeated itself again and again "on the same field of battle, between the same combatants." [31] In this unconcluded drama, the living had taken up the roles of the dead to carry on the "war of the past against the future," which admitted of neither truce nor neutrality and had enlisted the entire world under its banners.[32]

One of the most persistent characteristics of the revolutionary movement in nineteenth-century France was its heterogeneous composition. Blanqui was aware of the fact that the great popular uprisings always began with the proletarians fighting by the side of their class enemies in a popular front of bourgeois constitutionalists, radical republicans, socialist reformers, discontented workers, and communist revolutionaries, against an alliance of reactionaries who had never accepted the results of the first great Revolution, and conservatives who adhered to the results of the last one.

The triumph of the radical forces was always followed by an internecine struggle to define the nature of the new order. It was at this point that the fruits of the victory, won, Blanqui was convinced, by the fighting proletariat, were wrested from the workers by their bourgeois partners and despoilers. He observed that the bourgeois politicians

---

[31] Blanqui MSS, 9581, p. 2. The permanent revolution was seen by Proudhon as an idea which "had not ceased to grow in extent and to extend its conquests." Proudhon, *La Révolution au XIXe siècle*, p. 10.

[32] Blanqui MSS, 9591 (part 2), p. 321.

again and again had used the Parisian masses as their political catspaw:

They [the bourgeois politicians] place themselves at their [the workers] head, lead them in an attack on the government, take it over, entrench themselves, and from that moment, changed into conservatives, turn against this poor folk which becomes completely confused to see its generals of the eve become its tyrants on the morrow.[33]

This pattern of betrayal had ample precedent in the past, according to Blanqui's reading of history. The Hussites, the Jacquerie, the insurection of Étienne Marcel, were all doomed by the credulous faith which the masses put in the "moderates" who inevitably led them to destruction.[34] The Thermidorean reaction was the product of the bourgeois cowardice of legislatures established by the Revolution.[35] The Revolution of 1830 was betrayed by the opportunists who had inspired the people to destroy their Bourbon enemy.[36] The Revolution of 1848 had been delivered into the hands of the reaction by the so-called popular leaders, who parroted Jacobin and socialistic slogans until power was in their grasp.[37]

Blanqui's strongest public expression of his hatred for bourgeois democrats and socialist reformers was embodied in a toast upon the third anniversary of the February Revolution of 1848, entitled *Avis au Peuple,* which he sent to friends in England. This caustic personal denunciation of the *emigré* leaders of French radicalism—Ledru-Rollin, Louis Blanc, Crémieux, Lamartine, Garnier-Pagès, Dupont

---

[33] Quoted in Dommanget, *Blanqui à Belle-Ile,* p. 177 (from the letter to Maillard).

[34] Blanqui MSS, 9587, p. 354.

[35] *Ibid.,* 9590 (part 1), p. 66.

[36] *Ibid.,* 9592 (part 3), p. 20.

[37] Quoted in Dommanget, *Blanqui à Belle-Ile,* p. 174.

de l'Eure, Flocon, Albert, Arago, and Marrast—caused a sensation in European leftist circles. He brutally remarked that the blood of the victims of 1848 was upon the heads of these false "tribunes," and scornfully castigated the "forgetful indulgence" of the masses which once more turned them toward the very men who had led them to disaster.[38]

In answering the shocked reproaches occasioned by this diatribe, Blanqui warned against, "lulling the masses to sleep with this sad monotone of conciliatory moderatism." [39] It was ridiculous, he asserted in another letter, to let the leadership of the revolutionary opposition slip into the hands of the bourgeois republicans and thus "sacrifice the future to the unhealthy desire for an equivocal support in the present." [40]

This implacable combatant was perhaps the first Frenchman to define with brutal frankness what was to become the great dilemma of French socialism—to what degree might a socialist revolutionary "participate" in a political alliance with bourgeois and reformist elements? But merely to point out the danger of such an alliance does not resolve the problem for socialist participants in a mass rising against a reactionary government. Blanqui was ever searching for a means of distilling a proletarian and communist victory out of the vast undifferentiated dissent which was the necessary condition for the inception of a revolution.

He posed for himself the problem which was to become the great issue in Marxist controversy—how to transform the bourgeois revolution into a socialist victory, and a

[38] The *Avis au Peuple* is reproduced in Dommanget, *Blanqui à Belle-Ile*, pp. 64-66. A draft appears in the Blanqui MSS, 9581, pp. 11-13.

[39] Blanqui MSS, 9583, p. 416 (letter to Eduard, March, 1851).

[40] *Ibid.*, p. 398 (letter to Vidil, March, 1851).

coalition with the radical *petit bourgeoisie* and peasantry into a proletarian dictatorship.[41]   Actually Blanqui would not have phrased the problem in this manner—while Marx and his successors were concerned with transforming a middle-class revolution, Blanqui was attempting, when all of the conditions for this revolution were present, to anticipate it.

This crucial aspect of his political thought is expressed in these sentences: "if socialism is not its [the Revolution's] author it will not be its master.   It must make it, not allow it to be made.   The morrow belongs only to the victor." [42] In short, for a revolution to end in socialism, it had to be begun by socialists.   Blanqui believed, not that the elite could seize power without the support of the masses, but that the elite must launch an insurrection in order to assure the masses of the power they had so often won and then surrendered to the *bourgeoisie.*

This conception, expressed in 1853, should not be considered of much importance before that period.   The insurrection which Blanqui led in 1839 can probably be interpreted as a late fruit of Carbonarism and radical republicanism, at least in its motives and tactics.   In 1848 Blanqui operated in a manner much closer to Bolshevik practice—he eschewed immediate insurrection throughout

41 This, in a sense, is the idea of the "permanent revolution" which is sometimes attributed to Blanqui.   The French scholar, Charles Andler, writing about Marx, observed: "the circular of the Central Committee in 1850 prescribed a new tactic, the tactic of Blanqui, adopted by Marx, the 'permanent revolution.'   One must understand by this word a provisional coalition with the revolutionary *petite bourgeoisie,* for the entire period in which the majority will only be controlled by the revolutionary classes through this coalition."   C. Andler, *Le Manifeste Communiste* (Paris: F. Rieder et Cie., Éditeurs, n.d.), p. 136.

42 Blanqui MSS, 9583, p. 387.

most of the crisis and attempted to bring a steady pressure to bear on a weak and divided government until its power would drop into the hands of a stimulated and organized proletariat. After the disappointment of this hope Blanqui did apparently set himself the task of perfecting an organization which would be ready to act at the precise moment when economic maladjustment, popular discontent, and political passions were about to transform the mass potential which will overthrow the old order. His coup could not occur at any time, but only just in time to place the Hôtel de Ville in the hands of the proletarian vanguard.

L'Affaire de La Villette in August of 1870 was a perfect example of the practical consequences of this tactical aspiration.[43]   On that day Blanqui was persuaded, somewhat against his better judgement, to anticipate the revolution brewed out of Louis Napoleon's military defeats. This *attentat* petered out in the empty streets without having enlisted "a single recruit." [44]   Twenty-one days later the debacle of Sedan evoked the Parisian rising which destroyed the Empire and allowed Gambetta and his bourgeois colleagues to proclaim a new government at the Hôtel de Ville.

Blanqui criticized his own error with his usual unsparing candor. He had misjudged the moment, and in something so serious as a revolutionary enterprise, erroneous good intentions are unjustifiable. The same passage, however, expresses the assumptions behind his error: "the hour had not come; one must be able to predict it," [45] he wrote, demanding of himself a prescience which would allow him to fore-

[43] See pp. 153-54 above.

[44] Dommanget, *Blanqui, la guerre de 1870-71 et la Commune,* p. 114.

[45] Blanqui, *La Patrie en danger,* pp. 49-61.

tell the effective date of an uprising within considerably less than the three weeks which were the margin of his miscalculation on August 14, 1870.

THE REALPOLITIK OF UNSUCCESSFUL INSURRECTIONS

In a sense, Blanqui's fantasy of insurrection springs out of his harsh political realism. His preoccupation with power led him to the formulation of perhaps the first socialist *Realpolitik,* expressed in his slogan, "He who has arms has bread." [46] The impossibility of effecting a social program without political power is a truism, but one which Blanqui's socialist contemporaries (and many of his successors) characteristically ignored. Blanqui realized that so long as the coercive organs of the state were controlled by the conservatives, socialist ministries of public works, national workshops, and socialist parliamentary groups existed on sufferance.

This viewpoint is the measure of the gap between Blanquism and anarchism. True, he envisioned *L'Anarchie régulière* as the "future of humanity," [47] but he firmly believed that this Eldorado could only be attained through the instrumentality of the State. "The people can only escape from servitude through the impulsion of the great society of the state—for the state has no other legitimate mission." [48] The fact that the state was at present "the *gendarmerie* of the rich against the poor" [49] was no reason to reject the attempt to reverse this situation. The

[46] In the *Avis au Peuple,* in Dommanget, *Blanqui à Belle-Ile,* p. 66.
[47] Blanqui MSS, 9581, p. 23 (dated 1848). In this same passage, he wrote: "The government par excellence, the final goal of societies, is the absence of government."
[48] Blanqui, *Critique sociale,* II, 157-58.
[49] *Ibid.,* p. 146.

Proudhonian efforts to ignore the institution which was the agency for oppressing the workers and the hope of their freedom were the counsels of impotence.[50]

The immediate end of all Blanquist planning was the seizure of state power by the forces of the revolutionary vanguard. Force was the sole guarantee of liberty,[51] and "arms and organization" were the only means for securing the disarmament of the *bourgeoisie* and the arming of the masses—indispensable measures for the successful consummation of the revolution.[52]

It obviously follows from all this that the best-timed coup was fruitless without the most intensive prerevolutionary organization of a disciplined striking force. In 1869, Blanqui's characteristic ideas on this subject were elaborated in the *Instructions pour une prise d'armes,* wherein the first professional revolutionary attempted to draw up a technical manual for the profession.[53]

This analysis begins with a critique of revolutionary method as practiced by previous Parisian insurrectionists. The debacle of the Paris proletarist in June of 1848 was the final proof of the bankruptcy of their technique. "A Parisian insurrection based upon the old follies has today no further chance for success," he wrote, leading one momentarily to believe that he was repudiating his own political past. However, it develops that "the old follies" which he rejects are not those of insurrection as such, but the spontaneous, ill-organized mass surges which had marked the streetfighting of the past.

50 *Ibid.,* pp. 150-51.
51 Blanqui, "Instructions pour une prise d'armes," *Archiv fur die Geschichte des Arbeiterbewegung,* XV (1930), 276.
52 In the *Avis au Peuple,* in Dommanget, *Blanqui à Belle-Ile,* p. 66.
53 Blanqui, "Instructions pour une prise d'armes," *Archiv fur die Geschichte, Arbeiterbewegung,* XV (1930), 270-300.

Referring to the combatants of 1848, Blanqui wrote: "In order to get a clear idea of their defeat it suffices to analyze their strategy." This clearly expresses his unquenchable voluntarism—all of his observations about the long-run factor of social change never caused him to relinquish the idea that "revolutions . . . are made by men," [54] and that if revolutions fail, someone's planning is at fault.

Blanqui's own plans for coping with the troops, cannon, and chassepots of Louis Napoleon fell into three sections. First there is the clandestine agitation and propaganda among the masses undertaken simultaneously with the organization of the conspiracy and the formation of a pre-revolutionary cadre. Then, upon the chosen day, begins the insurrection and the application of plans for improvising a proletarian army in the very midst of the conflict. With this problem the *Instructions pour une prise d'armes* is primarily concerned. It analyzes in great deatil the combat functions of the elite, techniques for forming scratch fighting units, methods of erecting and defending barricades (with drawings), and a number of other practical requirements for winning a pitched battle for the control of Paris.

Blanqui introduces the third phase of his plan in the persons of a revolutionary hierarchy and its commander-in-chief. The leaders of the insurrection will exercise a battle-field dictatorship which will be transformed, upon a popular victory, into the "dictatorship of Paris." Blanqui never precisely states whether these two dictatorships are identical or how the executives of the Parisian dictatorship are to be chosen. We can probably assume that Blanqui thought of the Blanquist elite as identical, for all political purposes, with the Parisian "people" and worthy to rule in the name of Paris. On the other hand, there is little doubt that any

[54] Blanqui MSS, 9584 (part 1), pp. 116-17.

government chosen by the Paris masses during a revolution would have had considerable authority in Blanqui's
eyes.

Blanqui has often been credited with coining the phrase,
"the dictatorship of the proletariat," [55] but no one has ever
been able to document his use of it upon any occasion. We
have seen that his "dictatorship of Paris—the government of
the country by the country," may very well look backward
to Jacobin corruptions of Rousseau at least as much as
forward to Marx and Lenin.[56]

His rationalization of the political role of Paris we have
already considered. The reasons why this would be exercised in the form of a dictatorship are not far to seek.
The morrow of a revolution would find the *bourgeoisie* and
the other reactionaries defeated, but powerful and defiant,
and the peasant masses ignorant and misguided. The
revolutionaries would have to impose the measures which
could consolidate the gains of the revolution. The republican shibboleth of universal suffrage, which Blanqui had
taken up in his early days, was finally rejected as he came
to believe (and on the basis of good historical evidence) that
the countryside would tend to vote counterrevolutionaries
into office. Specifically, Blanqui fought against general
elections in 1848 and 1870, preferring a Paris government
dominated by his enemies among the *bourgeoisie* to an
assembly elected by the priest-ridden peasantry.[57]

For many years this dreaded conspirator actually defended, at least in the abstract, the standard position on
civil and political liberty.[58] He once wrote: "Liberty of

55 E.g., Postgate, "The Prisoner," *Out of the Past,* p. 54.
56 See pp. 165-66 above.   57 See pp. 139-40 above.
58 Blanqui once quoted Victor Hugo as having predicted that socialists would someday march with heads on their pikes, and then remarked that this type of activity was, in fact, "perfectly useless and

discussion is always without peril for justice and truth; it is only dangerous for iniquity and error. That is why iniquity and error, in their own defense, always have recourse to violence." [59]   Years of struggle however evoked the grim assertion that, "the day the gag comes out of the mouth of labor it will enter the mouth of capital." [60]   It was especially legitimate for an enlightened minority to end the dissemination of religious untruths by force, even if a majority had been deluded into accepting them.[61]   Blanqui's revolution would indeed "force the people to be free."

PLANS FOR POSTREVOLUTIONARY ORGANIZATION

Despite his distaste for postrevolutionary planning before the revolution, Blanqui outlined the minimal provisions for establishing his dictatorship.   The first concerns were with the maintenance of physical power—the arming of the workers, the wooing of neutralization of the army,[62] and the denial of power to bourgeois politicians.[63]   After these immediate tactical requirements few basic changes in the structure of society were envisaged.

The first task of the revolutionary police was, of course, the extirpation of all revealed religions.[64]   Along with the priests, the aristocrats, and those old enemies of the Repub-

---

rococo."   Blanqui MSS, 9591 (part 2), p. 547.   From time to time he did defend terrorism, but did not accept the position of the Blanquist Communards that the execution of hostages by the Commune was an act for which one should proudly assume the responsibility.   He wrote: "Now, if the death of the hostages and the police had been a great fault, this fault is the work of despair."   *Ibid.*, 9593, p. 34 (dated 1875).

[59] *Ibid.*, 9581, p. 53 (probably written in 1849 or 1850).

[60] Blanqui, *Critique sociale*, II, 208.

[61] Blanqui MSS, 9592 (part 1), pp. 142-43.

[62] *Ibid.*, 9591 (part 2), p. 293.

[63] *Ibid.*, 9583, p. 391.

[64] Blanqui, *Critique sociale*, II, 113.

lic whose political crimes dated from 1848 [65] were to be driven from the land. The army was to be replaced by a national militia, all but the most junior civil servants were to be removed, and the entire magistrature scrapped for a universal system of trial by jury.[66] There is no hint of socialism among these "immediate dispositions" and not much more is to be found in Blanqui's specific provisions for the "economic order."

Some economic regulation was immediately necessary in order to maintain production against the traditional capitalist tactic of withdrawing funds from the economic stream in order to coerce a hostile government. Aside from the swift and sharp punishments which were to inhibit such a course, and the expropriation of church lands, Blanqui's initial economic reforms were moderate indeed. They included progressive taxes, the regulation of credit, exports, imports, and some national monopolies; and the organization of national "worker's associations." Private property was to remain untouched at first, for Blanqui, true to his theory that universal enlightenment was the prerequisite of communism, felt that a revolutionary government could only proceed against capitalism with the greatest caution until such a time as the peasants understood communism, "not as a menace but as a hope." [67]

Eventually universal education would open people's eyes to the manifest benefits of economic association. Here the intransigent revolutionary sounds a note of optimism on the persuadability of the French peasant-proprietor that could swell the chorus of Blanc, Cabet, and Fourier. Blanqui's dictatorship was to change the economic institutions of a

[65] *Ibid.*, I, 205. He also suggested the annulment of all property sales which had occurred since Feb. 24, 1848. This is historicism with a vengeance.

[66] *Ibid.*   [67] *Ibid.*, p. 210.

nation by controlling its political machinery long enough to educate it.   This is the ultimate product of his social idealism—the assurance that the state could effect a proletarian revolution in the minds of the people in the midst of capitalist economic institutions.

In all probability the uncompromising activist would have preferred not to be judged on the basis of his plans for postrevolutionary consolidation.   The only chance that he might have had for a practical application of his postrevolutionary plans—that is, the Paris Commune of 1870—was denied to him by Thiers's police.

Many writers have found the supreme irony of Blanqui's life in his enforced absence from the Commune.   He had, in a sense, spent his life preparing for that event.   According to Marx [68] and others he was the natural leader of its combatants, yet he found himself a helpless prisoner throughout this poorly led campaign against his lifelong enemies.

The real irony, however, lies not in his absence from the Commune, but in the fact that the Commune represented the actual consummation of his political ideas—that is, the seizure of Paris by a militarized organization of armed workers led by the left wing of the radical movement—and that this "success" was, in fact, the occasion for a decisive and bloody defeat of French radicalism.

[68] K. Marx, *The Civil War in France* (Chicago: Charles H. Kerr and Co., 1934), p. 116.   Postgate went so far as to write: "With Blanqui the Commune could, without question, have defeated Thiers and taken Versailles."   Postgate, *Out of the Past*, p. 50.

CHAPTER NINE

Conclusion: The Revolution as Will and Idea

IN THE EYES OF most men, the sole justification for a revolution is its success. In the words of Stendhal, "what is more repulsive than an unsuccessful Jacobin?" [1] Thus, Blanqui's place in history is often defined by his political failures, and he is dismissed as the type of sinister adventurer desiring violence for its own sake.[2]

Historians like Arthur Rosenberg, who describes Blanqui as "the living conscience of French democracy," [3] or Raymond Postgate, who sees in the Frenchman " a leader only less in importance than Marx," [4] are saying, in effect, that his unhappy record of abortive insurrection was transcended by the influence of his personality or his ideas.

The profundity or the priority of Blanqui's ideas can be exaggerated, but their influence upon many generations of the French left, and their perpetuation in certain aspects of European socialism, is undeniable. Certain conceptions, which Blanqui expressed at a relatively early date in the history of modern socialism, are taken for granted as theoretical foundations of the "revolutionary" branch of that movement.

The most important of these are: the assertion of the inseparable nature of socialist reform and political revolu-

[1] Stendhal, *Scarlet and Black*, tr. M. R. B. Shaw (London: Penguin Books, 1953), p. 301.

[2] E.g., G. Elton, *The Revolutionary Idea in France 1789-1871* (New York: Longmans, Green and Co., 1923), p. 152.

[3] Rosenberg, *Democracy and Socialism*, p. 94.

[4] Postgate, *Out of the Past*, p. 31.

tion; the characterization of political struggle as, historically, a conflict of economic classes, distinguished by their
relationship to the means of production; the rejection of
any long-term collaboration between proletarian revolutionaries and bourgeois reformers; and the stress upon the
revolutionary will as the basic agent of progress, and its
immediate manifestation in the conquest of physical power.

Blanqui's lifelong endeavor to apply the most extreme
political consequences of eighteenth-century rationalism to
nineteenth-century society made him, in a way, the personification of the intellectual development of revolutionary
socialism in the first two-thirds of the nineteenth century.[5]
He came to economic reform through his early dedication
to political revolution. He was a middle-class intellectual
whose political disappointments led him to identify progress
with the proletariat. He was an activist who never freed
himself from the Utopianism he so explicitly rejected, mix-
ing a sense of the glacier-like movement of historical forces
with the belief that the perfection of Man could be advanced into the foreseeable future through the actions of a
few enlightened men.

To recognize the significance of Blanquist theory is not
to establish Blanqui as primarily a theorist. He was first
of all a man of action, but he justified that action by what
he felt to be a thoroughgoing rationalism based upon systematic thought and extensive reading. This justification
is characteristically derived from "self-evident" principles
which he did not always bother to define and is most often
developed as an *ad hoc* polemic which sacrifices logical re-
finement to immediate political ends.

[5] We cannot precisely agree with Neil Stewart's observation that,
"In the life of Blanqui we see the whole history of the development
of the working class in the nineteenth century." Stewart, *Blanqui,*
p. 288.

His very commitment to direct action impels us, in some degree, to judge his theories according to the standard of practical accomplishment. Blanquism was not an academic analysis, but a diagnosis which was to indicate the cure for a society already assumed to be diseased. Failure in practice, as Blanqui would have been the first to admit, implied theoretical error, and the reasons for the practical failure illuminate the weaknesses of the theory.

The commonest criticism of Blanquism decries its voluntarist ignorance of the historical factors which delimit the boundaries of practicable social enterprise at any particular moment. There is ample evidence, however, that the conspirator himself never ceased to pay theoretical homage, at least, to the inexorable constraints which slowly maturing social and economic conditions place upon revolutionary endeavors.[6] It is in his definition of the objective conditions of successful insurrection that we can discern one source of his sterile practice. As the historian Rudolf Schlesinger has acutely observed, "in the Blanquist concept the only objective condition regarded as necessary is a general state of society so desperate that a sufficiently strong elite finds it worthwhile to wager everything for the sake of its overthrow, and may expect mass-sympathies for its attempts at social reconstruction."[7]

From this follows the emphasis upon the subjective conditions of a proletarian victory. No group of men can make a revolutionary situation, but when it exists, some men will distill power from it. Blanquism was the resolution to forestall the enemies, and the false friends of the proletariat by being the first and best organized group

6 See p. 145 above.
7 R. Schlesinger, *Marx, His Time and Ours* (London: Routledge, 1950), p. 255.

upon the day when the inevitable transfer of political power should occur.

The consequence of this viewpoint is that putschism for which Blanqui is so often condemned. He would have preferred to lead the great mass of the proletariat against its class enemies, but his conception of the Revolution as Will and Idea could only be carried out by that small group which embodied both. The enlightened elite had to cut itself off from the masses, in the name of whom it was to destroy the political superstructure of capitalist oppression, in order to be certain of the discipline, secrecy, and resolution required by insurrection.

We have remarked that this tactic is not necessarily justified by a reference to the political conditions which made legal dissent, especially when it was socialistic, hazardous, if not impossible. Under similar conditions more successful movements have maintained coherence and a minimum of secrecy while developing techniques such as the constant identification with popular economic aspirations, the infiltration of mass organizations, and the skillful use of available means of legal agitation and propaganda, which Blanqui hardly envisaged.

The relevance of such a comparison is limited by the fact that historical analogy is tenuous at best. The differences between the Bolshevist milieu and the world of Blanqui are more significant than their similarities. We might observe that one difference was the Bolshevist knowledge of the history of Blanquism.

It may be that any consideration of Blanquist methods tells us little about his practical failure that is not already implied by the anachronistic nature of his goals. Blanqui was an important link between the Jacobin tradition and modern revolutionary socialism, but he was both too early and too late for the fruition of his own hopes. His dream of world progress through the force of an enlightened Paris was already out of date in 1830. His conception of a proletarian commonwealth was expressed in an era when the world proletariat was infinitely weaker than its most cautious prophets would allow themselves to believe, and in a nation whose working class remained a small minority of the total population.

The last statement must, perhaps, be qualified in the light of recent history. Leftist politics born of conspiracy and violence have not triumphed in those nations with a large, highly organized industrial proletariat, but in the lands where a vast peasant majority clung to a marginal existence under semifeudal conditions of economic organization. Perhaps, Blanqui's projects were so Utopian, not because the French working class was numerically weak, but because the Revolution, from which he drew his political inspiration, had guaranteed the existence of a rural class which has remained the bulwark of French capitalism.

In Blanqui's disastrous commitment to permanent rebellion is the germ of his influence upon socialist theory. He was probably the first to consider social revolution, not as an *ad hoc* problem, but as an art, a profession, and a social science; and seriously to pose those questions: What constitutes a revolutionary situation? Who shall reap its fruit? What are the tactics of successful insurrection?—which are today the preoccupation of gigantic contending forces.

Bibliography

THE UNPUBLISHED WRITINGS OF LOUIS AUGUSTE BLANQUI

Bibliothèque Nationale, Blanqui MSS, Nouvelles acquisitions françaises, 9578–9598.

THE PUBLISHED WRITINGS OF LOUIS AUGUSTE BLANQUI

L'Armée esclave et opprimée. Paris: Imprimerie du Passage de l'Opera, 1880.

Aux étudiants en médecine et en droit. Paris: Imprimerie de H. Fournier, 1830.

Critique sociale. 2 vols. Paris: Félix Alcan, 1885.

Déclaration adoptée par le Comité des Écoles sur la présentation d'Auguste Blanqui. 1831.

Défense du citoyen L. A. Blanqui devant la Cour d'assises. Paris: Imprimerie Auguste Mie, 1832.

Départ des prisonniers de Vincennes, leur adieux au peuple, derniers paroles des citoyens Barbès, Raspail, Blanqui et Hubert, addressées au President de la République Louis Napoleon. 1849.

"Un Dernier mot par L. A. Blanqui," *Le Châtiment,* March 3, 1871. (A broadside.)

L'Éternité par les astres. Paris: Librairie Germer Baillière, 1872.

Foi et Science ou la science du R. P. Gratry par "Suzamel." Bruxelles: Typographie de D. Bresmee, 1866. (This is the collection of Blanqui's anticlerical articles from the newspaper, *Candide.*)

"Instructions pour une prise d'armes," *Archiv fur die Geschichte des Arbeiterbewegung,* XV (1930), pp. 270-300. (With an introduction and notes by Georges Bourgin.)

Izbriannye Proizvedeniio. Translated by F. B. Shuvayef (with an introduction by V. P. Volgin). Moscow: Academy of Sciences SSR, 1952.

Letters to Mlle Montgolfier. *Les Lettres,* Première Année, Nos. VII and VIII, (1906).

La Patrie en danger. Paris: A. Chevalier, 1871. (A collection of Blanqui's articles from his newspaper, *La Patrie en danger*).

Propagande démocratique (with Hadot-Desages). Paris: Imprimerie de L. E. Derhan.

Résponse du citoyen Auguste Blanqui. Paris: Imprimerie d'Ad. Blondeau, 1848.

The following Blanquist newspapers are important sources of his published ideas:

    Le Libérateur, 1834
    Candide, 1866
    La Patrie en danger, 1870-1871
    Ni Dieu Ni Maître, 1880-1881

Other important writings have been published in:

Dommanget, Maurice. Blanqui à Belle-Ile. Paris: Librairie du Travail, 1935.

Mathiez, Albert. "Notes de Blanqui sur Robespierre," *Annales Historiques de la Révolution Française,* V (July-Aug., 1928), 305-21.

Silvestre, Théophile. L. A. Blanqui, études historiques, pièces justificatives. Paris: Librairie Poulet-Malassis, 1862.

Zévaès, Alexandre, "Pages inédites de Blanqui (1848-1852)," *La Révolution de 1848,* XXII (1925-26), 541-58.

DOCUMENTS—OFFICIAL AND SEMI-OFFICIAL

Commission d'Enquête. Pièces relatives aux événements du 15 Mai et l'insurrection de Juin. Bordeaux: Imprimerie Durand.

Compte Rendu de l'affaire du 15 Mai.

Cours des Pairs. Affaire des 12 et 13 Mai, 1839. Paris: Imprimerie Royal, 1839.

La Gazette des Tribunaux.

Le Moniteur Universel.

Société des Amis du Peuple. Procès des Quinze. Paris: Imprimerie de Auguste Mie, 1832.

NEWSPAPERS

L'Ami du Peuple en 1848, 1848

La Commune de Paris, 1848
Le XIXᵉ Siècle, 1879
L'Égalité, 1878
Le Journal, 1896
La Marseillaise, 1879
Opinion Nationale, 1872
Paris-Journal, 1872
Le Peuple, 1848
Le Populaire, 1848
Le Prolétaire, 1879
La Réforme (Lyon), 1879
Le Représentant du Peuple, 1848
République Française, 1872
La Révolution Française, 1879
The Times (London), 1879
Les Veillées du Peuple, 1849-1850
La Voix des Clubs, 1848

BOOKS AND ARTICLES BY OTHER AUTHORS

Albringues, E. Discours anniversaire de Blanqui. Toulouse: Imprimerie Lagout et Sebille, 1898.

Alibert, A. A. Blanqui. Nîmes: G. Terssier, 1911.

Andler, Charles. Le Manifeste Communiste. Paris: F. Rieder et Cie., Editeurs, n.d.

Arendt, Hannah. The Origins of Totalitarianism. New York: Harcourt, Brace and Co., 1951.

Barbès, J. A. "Notice sur la vie d'Armand Barbès," La Révolution de 1848, II (1905-6), 209-19.

Bastiat, Fréderic. Essays on Political Economy. Translated by David A. Wells. New York: G. P. Putnam and Sons, 1877.

Bauer, Henry. Mémoires d'un jeune homme. Paris: Bibliothèque-Charpentier, 1895.

Bernard. Curiosités révolutionnaires. Paris: O. Giraud et J. Dagneau, Librairies-Editeurs, 1851.

Bernard, Martin. Dix ans de prison au Mont-Saint-Michel et à la citadelle de Doullens, 1839 à 1848. Paris: Pagnerre, Librairie-Éditeur, 1861.

Bernstein, Eduard. Socialisme théorique et Social Démocratie pratique. Translated by A. Cohen. Paris: P. V. Stock, 1900.

Bernstein, Samuel. The Beginnings of Marxian Socialism in France. New York: Social Science Studies, 1933.

—— Buonarroti. Translated (into French) by M. Gilles. Grandes Figures Hier et Aujourd'hui.

—— "Marx in Paris, 1848: A Neglected Chapter," *Science and Society*, Summer, 1939, pp. 323-55.

Blanc, Louis. Appel aux honnêtes gens. Paris: Au Bureau Central, 1849.

—— 1848. Historical Revelations. London: Chapman and Hall, 1858.

—— Histoire de la Révolution de 1848. Vol. II. Paris: Librairie Internationale, 1870.

—— History of Ten Years. Vol. I. London: Chapman and Hall, 1844.

Blanqui, Jérôme Adolphe. "Souvenirs d'un étudiant sous la Restauration," *Revue de Paris* (Nov.-Dec., 1918), pp. 158-76.

Bourgin, Georges. La Commune. Paris: Les Éditions Nationales, 1939.

Bourgin, Georges, and Hubert Bourgin. Le Socialisme français de 1789 à 1848. Paris: Hachette et Cie., 1912.

Bouton, Victor. Profil révolutionnaire de L. A. Blanqui par un crayon rouge. Paris: Victor Bouton Editeur, 1849.

Byrnes, Robert F. Anti-Semitism in Modern France. New Brunswick: Rutgers University Press, 1950.

Cahen, L. "L'Idée de lutte des classes au XVIIIe siècle," *Revue de synthèse historique*, XII (Jan.-June, 1906), pp. 44-56.

Callet, A. "Un grand patriote méconnu. Auguste Blanqui," *La Nouvelle Revue*, XXXV (May-June, 1918), pp. 111-18.

Calman, Alvin R. Ledru-Rollin and the Second French Republic. New York: Columbia University Press, 1922.

Calmette, M. A. "Les Carbonari en France," *La Révolution de 1848*, IX (1912-13), 401-17, and X (1913-14), 52-73, 117-37, 214-30.

Castille, Hippolyte. Histoire de la Seconde République française, 4 vols. Paris: Victor Lecou, 1854-56.

—— "L. A. Blanqui," in Portraits politiques et historiques au dix-neuvième siècle. Paris: Ferdinand Sartorius, 1857.

Caussidière. Mémoires. Vol. II. Paris: Michel Levy, 1849.

Chenu, A. Les Conspirateurs. Paris: Garnier Freres, 1850.

Clapham, J. H. The Economic Development of France and Germany, 1815-1914. Cambridge: University Press, 1951.

Cole, G. D. H. Socialist Thought, the Forerunners 1789-1850. London: MacMillan and Co., 1953.

Combes, Louis. Portraits révolutionnaires—Blanqui. Paris: Madre Éditeur, 1892.

Compère-Morel, and Charles Rappaport. Un Peu d'histoire, Vol. I of Encylopédie Socialiste. Edited by Compére-Morel. Paris-Aristide Quillet, 1912.

Condorcet, Esquisse d'un tableau historique des progrès de l'esprit humain. Paris: Masson et Fils, 1822.

Corcelle, Francois de. Documents pour servir a l'histoire des conspirations. Paris: Paulin, 1831.

Cornu, Auguste. Karl Marx et la Révolution de 1848. Paris: Presses Universitaires de France, 1948.

Da Costa, Charles. Les Blanquistes, Vol. VI of Histoires des partis socialistes en France. Paris: Marcel Rivière, 1912.

De la Hodde, Lucien. Histoire des sociétés secrètes et du parti républicain. Paris: Julien, Lanier et Cie., 1850.

Delevsky, J. Les Antinomies Socialistes. Paris: Marcel Giard, 1930.

Delord, Taxile. Histoire du Second Empire. Paris: Librairie Germen Baillière, 1873.

Delvau, Alfred. Histoire de la Révolution de Février. Paris: Garnier Frères, 1850.

Dessal, Marcel. Charles Delescluze. Paris: Librairie Marcel Rivière et Cie., 1952.

Deville, Gabriel. "Blanqui," in La Grande Encyclopédie. Lamuault et Cie., Éditeurs. Vol. VI.

—— Blanqui Libre. Paris: Typographie G. Deville, 1878.

Doctrine Saint Simonienne—Exposition. Paris: Librairie Nouvelle, 1854.

Dommanget, Maurice. "L'Athéisme et l'anti-catholicisme de Blanqui," Bulletin Rationaliste, July, 1952.

—— "Auguste Blanqui et l'insurrection du 12 Mai 1839," La Critique Sociale, XI (March, 1934), 233-45.

—— Blanqui. Paris: Librairie de l'Humanité, 1924.

Dommanget (continued)
—— Blanqui à Belle-Ile. Paris: Librairie du Travail, 1935.
—— "Blanqui et le document Tascherau. Les 'faveurs' de Blanqui," 1848, Revue des Révolutions Contemporaines (July, 1950), pp. 137-66.
—— Blanqui, la Guerre de 1870-71 et la Commune. Paris: Éditions Domat, 1947.
—— Une drame politique en 1848. Paris: Les Deux Sirènes, 1948.
—— "Les Groupes Blanquistes de la fin du Second Empire," Revue Socialiste, XLIV (Feb., 1951), 225-31.
—— Hommes et choses de la Commune. Marseille: Editions de la Coopérative des Amis de "L'École Émancipée," 1937.
—— Pages choisies de Babeuf. Paris: Librairie Armand Colin, 1935.
Dubreilh, Louis. In Jean Juarès, La Guerre Franco-Allemande; and Louis Dubreilh, La Commune. Vol. XI of Histoire Socialiste. Edited by Jean Jaurès. Paris: Publications Jules Rouff et Cie., 1906.
Dupont, Étienne. Les Prisons du Mont Saint-Michel. Paris: Perrin et Cie., 1913.
Duquai, E. Les Grands procès politiques—les accusés du 15 Mai 1848. Paris: Armand Le Chevalier, 1869.
Eastman, Max. Marx and Lenin. New York: Albert and Charles Boni, 1927.
Elton, G. The Revolutionary Idea in France 1789-1871. New York: Longmans, Green and Co., 1923.
Emden, Paul H. Money Powers of Europe in the Nineteenth and Twentieth Century. London: Sampson Low, Marston and Co., Ltd., 1937.
Engels, Friedrich, and Karl Marx. Historisch–Kritische Gesamtausgabe. Third Division, Vols. I, III, IV. Berlin: Marx–Engels Verlag, 1931.
—— "History of the Communist League," in Germany: Revolution and Counter Revolution. New York: International Publishers, 1933.
—— Ludwig Feuerbach—and the Outcome of Classical German Philosophy. Vol. XV of Marxist Library, Works of Marxism–Leninism. New York: International Publishers, n.d.

—— "The Program of the Blanquist Fugitives from the Paris Commune," in Karl Marx, The Civil War in France. Chicago: Charles H. Kerr and Co., 1934.

Flotte, Benjamin. Blanqui et les otages en 1871. Paris: Imprimerie Jeannette, 1885.

Forni, Jules. Raoul Rigault. Paris: Librairie Centrale, 1871.

Fournière, Eugène. La Règne de Louis Philippe, Vol. VIII of Histoire Socialiste. Edited by Jean Jaures. Paris: Publications Jules Rouff et Cie., 1906.

Garaudy, Roger. "Le Néo-blanquisme de contrebande et les positions antiléninistes d'André Marty," *Cahiers du Communisme* (Jan., 1953), pp. 38-50.

—— Les Sources françaises du socialisme scientifique. Paris: Éditions Hier et Aujourd'hui, 1948.

Garnier–Pagès. Histoire de la Révolution de 1848. 8 vols. Paris: Pagnerre, 1861.

Garrone, Alessandro Galante. Fillipo Buonarroti e i revoluzionari dell' ottocento (1828-1837). Turin: Biblioteca di cultura storica, 1951.

Geffroy, Gustave L'Enfermé. 2 vols. Paris: Les Éditions G. Crès et Cie., 1926.

Girard, Fulgence. Histoire du Mont Saint-Michel. Paris: Paul Permain et Cie., 1849.

Guest, David. A Textbook of Dialectical Materialism. New York: International Publishers, 1939.

Guillon, E. Les Complots militaires sous la Restauration. Paris: Librairie Plon, 1895.

Hayes, Carlton J. H. The Historical Evolution of Modern Nationalism. New York: The Macmillan Co., 1948.

Heine, Heinrich. French Affairs, Letters from Paris. Translated by C. G. Leland. London: W. Heinemann, 1893.

Holbach, Baron d'. La Politique naturelle. London: 1773.

Hugo, Victor. Choses Vues. 2 vols. Paris: La Librairie Ollendorff, 1913.

—— Souvenirs Personnels, 1848-1851. Edited by H. Guillemin. Paris: Gallimard, 1952.

Isambert, Gaston. Les Idées socialistes en France de 1815 à 1848. Paris: Félix Alcan Editeur, 1905.

Jaurès, Jean. L'Armée nouvelle. Paris: Publications Jules Rouff et Cie., 1911.

—— La Guerre Franco–Allemande; and Louis Dubreuilh. La Commune. Vol. XI of Histoire Socialiste. Edited by Jean Jaurès. Paris: Publications Jules Rouff et Cie., 1906.

—— Oeuvres. Edited by Max Bonnafour. Vol. III. Paris: Les Editions Rieder, 1931.

Jeanjean, J. F. Armand Barbès. Vol. I. Paris: Édouard Cornély et Cie., 1909.

Karpovich, Michael. "A Forerunner of Lenin, P. N. Tkatchev," *Review of Politics* IV (July, 1944), 336-50.

Kautsky, Karl. Krieg und Demokratie. Vol. I. Berlin: Verlag J. H. W. Dietz, 1932.

Kenafick, K. J. Michael Bakunin and Karl Marx. Melbourne: Hawthorn Press, 1948.

Labusquière, John. La Troisième République. Vol. XII of Histoire Socialiste. Edited by Jean Jaurès. Paris: Publications Jules Rouff et Cie., 1906.

Lafargue, Paul. "A Blanqui souvenirs personnel," *La Révolution Française,* April 20, 1879.

Lamartine, Alphonse de. Histoire de la Révolution de 1848. Vol. I. Leipzig: Brockhaus & Avenarius, 1849.

Lange, Frederick A. The History of Materialism. Translated by Ernest Chester Thomas. 3 vols. in one. New York: Harcourt, Brace and Co., 1925.

Lebey, A. "Blanqui et Raspail à Doullens en 1849," *La Révolution de 1848,* VII (1910-11), 181-95.

Lefrançais, Gustave. Souvenirs d'un révolutionnaire. Bruxelles: Imprimerie Ch. Hautstont, 1902.

Lenin, V. I. "K Itogam S'ezda" (The Congress Summed Up), in Vol. IX of Sochineniia. 3d ed. Moscow: Giz, 1935.

—— Materialism and Empirico-Criticism. Vol. XIII of Collected Works of V. I. Lenin. New York: International Publishers, 1927.

—— On the Eve of October. Vol. XIII of Little Lenin Library. New York: International Publishers, 1932.

—— Religion. Vol. VII of Little Lenin Library. New York: International Publishers, 1933.

—— "What Is to Be Done?" Marx–Engels–Marxism. Moscow: Foreign Languages Publishing House, 1947.

Lepper, John Heron. Famous Secret Societies. London: Sampson Low, Marston and Co.

Leroy, Maxime. Les Précurseurs français du socialisme. Paris: Éditions du Temps Présent, 1948.

Leymarie, Camille. "Barbès et Blanqui a Belle-Ile," La Nouvelle Revue, XV (June 1, 1898), 385-95.

Lissagaray. Histoire de la Commune de 1871. Paris: Librairie Marcel Rivière et Cie., 1947.

Louis, Paul. Cent Cinquante Ans de pensée socialiste. Paris: Librairie Marcel Riviere et Cie., 1947.

—— Histoire du socialisme en France 1789–1945. Paris: Librairie Marcel Rivière et Cie., 1946.

Lucas, Alphonse. Les Clubs et les clubistes. Paris: E. Dentu, 1851.

Malon, Benoît. "Blanqui Socialiste," Revue Socialiste, II (July, 1885), 586-97.

Marty, André. Quelques Aspects de l'activité de Blanqui. Paris: Société des Amis de Blanqui, 1951.

Marx, Karl. The Civil War in France. Chicago: Charles H. Kerr and Co., 1934.

—— The Class Struggles in France. New York: International Publishers, 1935.

—— A Contribution to the Critique of Political Economy. Translated by N. I. Stone. New York: The International Library Publishing Co., 1904.

—— "The Eighteenth Brumaire of Louis Bonaparte," in Vol. II of Selected Works. Edited by Victor Adoratsky. New York: International Publishers, 1939.

—— "On the Jewish Question," Selected Essays. Translated by H. J. Stenning. New York: International Publishers, 1926.

Marx, Karl, and Friedrich Engels. Historisch–Kritische Gesamtausgabe. Third Division, Vols. I, III, IV. Berlin: Marx–Engels Verlag, 1931.

—— "Manifesto of the Communist Party," in Selected Works. Moscow: Foreign Languages Publishing House, 1950.

—— Selected Correspondence. Vol. XXIX of Marxist Library. New York: International Publishers, 1932.

Mason, Edward, S. "Blanqui and Communism," *Political Science Quarterly*, XLIV (Dec. 1929), 498-527.

—— The Paris Commune. New York: Macmillan Co., 1930.

Mathiez, Albert. "Notes de Blanqui sur Robespierre," *Annales Historiques de la Révolution Française*, V (July-Aug., 1928), 305-21.

Mayer, J. P. Political Thought in France. London: Rutledge and Kegan Paul Ltd., 1949.

Megaro, G. Mussolini in the Making. London: George Allen and Unwin Ltd., 1938.

Mehring, Franz. Karl Marx. New York: Covici-Friede, 1935.

Memoirs of the Secret Societies of the South of Italy, Particularly the Carbonari. London: John Murray, 1821.

Ménard, Louis. Lettres inédites. Edited by Henry Peyre. Paris: Presses Universitaires de France, 1932.

Menger, Karl. Principles of Economics. Translated by Dingwall and Hoselitz. Glencoe: The Free Press, 1950.

Mirecourt, Eugène de. Blanqui. Vol. XVI of Les Contémporains. Paris: Chez l'auteur. 1857.

Molinier, Sylvain. Blanqui. Paris: Presses Universitaires de France, 1948.

Monin, M. "Blanqui et la police 1847–1848," *La Révolution de 1848*, XII (1915-16), 26-38.

Morange, G. Les Idées communistes dans les sociétés secrètes et dans la presse sous la Monarchie de Juillet. Paris: V. Giard and E. Briere, 1905.

Les Murailles révolutionnaires. Paris: J. Bry Ainè, 1852.

Neumann, Franz. Behemoth. New York. Oxford University Press, 1944.

Nicolaievsky, Boris and Otto Maenchen-Helfen. Karl Marx. Translated by G. David and E. Mosbacher. Philadelphia: J. B. Lippincott Co., 1936.

Noguès, L. Une Condamnation de Mai 1839. Paris: J. Bry Ainé, 1850.

Nomad, Max. Apostles of Revolution. Boston: Little, Brown and Co., 1939.

Parker, Harold T. The Cult of Antiquity and the French Revolutionaries. Chicago, The University of Chicago Press, 1937.

Perreux, Gabriel. Au Temps des sociétés secrètès. Paris: Librairie Hachette, 1931.

Picard, R. Le Romantisme social. New York: Brentano's, 1944.

Plamenatz, John. The Revolutionary Movement in France, 1815-1871. London: Longmans, Green and Co., 1952.

Plotkin, Norman. "Les Alliances des Blanquistes dans la proscrition," 1848, Revue des Revolutions Contemporaines (Dec., 1951), 116-21.

Pompery, Édouard de. Blanquisme et Opportunisme. Paris: Auguste Ghio, Éditeur, 1879.

Postgate, Raymond W. The Bolshevik Theory. New York: Dodd, Mead and Co., 1920.

—— How to Make A Revolution. New York: The Vanguard Press, 1934.

—— "The Prisoner," in Out of the Past. London: The Labour Publishing Co., Ltd., 1922.

—— Revolution from 1789 to 1906. New York: Houghton Mifflin Co., 1921.

Prelot, Marcel. L'Évolution politique du socialisme français, 1789-1934. Paris: Éditions Spes, 1939.

Proudhon, P. J. Les Confessions d'un révolutionnaire. Paris: Au bureau du journal La Voix du Peuple, 1849.

—— Lettres au Citoyen Rolland. Edited by J. Bompard. Paris: Éditions Bernard Grasset, 1946.

—— La Révolution au XIXe siècle. Paris: Garnier Frères, 1851.

Puech, Jules, L. Le Proudhonisme dans l'Association International des Travailleurs. Paris: Felix Alcan, 1907.

Ralea, M. L'Idée de révolution dans les doctrines socialistes. Paris: Jouve et Cie., 1923.

Ranc, Arthur. Souvenirs—Correspondance 1831-1908. Paris: Édouard Cornély et Cie., 1913.

Rappaport, Charles, and Compère-Morel. Un Deu d'histoire, Vol. I of Encyclopédie Socialiste. Edited by Compere-Morel. Paris: Aristide Quillet, 1912.

Regnault, Élias. Histoire du Gouvernement Provisoire. Paris: Victor Lecou, 1850.

Renard, Georges. "Une lettre relative au document Taschereau," La Révolution de 1848, VII (1910-11), 7-15.

Renard (*continued*)

—— La République de 1848, Vol. IX of Histoire Socialiste. Edited by Jean Jaurès. Paris: Publications Jules Rouff et Cie., 1906.

Revue Retrospective. Paris: Paulin, 1848.

Robiquet, Paul. Buonarroti. Paris: Librairie Hachette et Cie., 1910.

Rosenberg, Arthur. Democracy and Socialism. Translated by G. Roben. New York: Alfred A. Knopf, 1939.

Scheurer-Kestner, Auguste. Souvenirs de jeunesse. Paris: Bibliothèque-Charpentier, 1905.

Schirokauer, Arno. Lassalle. Translated by Edan and Cedar Paul. London: George Allen and Unwin Ltd., 1931.

Schlesinger, Rudolf. Marx, His Time and Ours. London: Routledge, 1950.

Sée, Henri. Histoire économique de la France. Vol. II. Paris: Librairie Armand Colin, 1942.

Seignobos, Charles. La Révolution de 1848—Le Second Empire, Vol. VI of Histoire de France contemporaine. Edited by E. Lavisse. Paris: Librairie Hachette, 1921.

Sencier, Georges. Le Babouvisme après Babeuf. Paris: Marcel Rivière et Cie., 1912.

Sénés. "Blanqui," in Provenceaux—Notes Biographiques. Toulon, 1904.

Simon, F. L. A. Blanqui en Anjou. Angers: Cooperative Imprimerie Angevine, 1939.

Sombart, Werner. Socialism and the Social Movement. Translated by M. E. Epstein. New York: E. P. Dutton and Co., 1919.

Stern, Daniel (Mme D'Agoult). Histoire de la Révolution de 1848. 3 Vols. Paris: Calmann Lévy, 1878.

Stewart, Neil. Blanqui. London: Victor Gollancz Ltd., 1939.

Szajkowski, Z. "The Jewish St. Simonians and Socialist Anti-Semitism in France," *Jewish Social Studies,* IX (Jan., 1947), 33-60.

Tchernoff, J. L'Extrême-Gauche socialiste-révolutionnaire en 1870-71. Paris: Bureaux de l'Action Nationale, 1918.

—— Le Parti républicain au coup d'état et sous le Second Empire. Paris: A. Pedone, 1906.

—— Le Parti républicain sous la Monarchie de Juillet. Paris: A. Pedone, 1901.

Thomas, Albert. Le Second Empire. Vol. X of Histoire Social-iste. Edited by J. Jaurès. Paris: Publications Jules Rouff et Cie., 1906.

Thomson, David. Democracy in France. London: Oxford University Press, 1946.

Tocqueville, Alexis de. Recollections. Translated by A. T. de Mattos, New York: Columbia University Press, 1949.

Toussenel, Alphonse. Histoire de la féodalité financière, les juifs rois de l'époque. Paris: Gabriel de Conet, 1847.

Trélat. "La Charbonnerie," in Paris révolutionnaire. Vol. II. Paris: Chez Guillaumin, 1834.

Tridon, Gustav. Les Hébertistes. Paris: Chez L'Auteur, 1864.

Vallès, Jules. L'Insurgé. Paris: Bibliothèque-Charpentier, 1914.

Wasserman, Suzanne. Les Clubs de Barbès et de Blanqui. Paris: Édouard Cornély et Cie., 1913.

[Watteau.] Blanqui devant les révélations historiques; par R——. Bruxelles: Vve. Verteneuil, 1859.

Weill, Georges. Histoire du parti républicain en France (1814-1870). Paris: Librairie Félix Alcan, 1928.

Weulersse, G. Les Physiocrates. Paris: Gaston Doin et Cie., 1931.

Whittaker, E. A History of Economic Ideas. New York: Long-mans, Green and Co., 1940.

Zévaès, Alexandre, Auguste Blanqui. Paris: Marcel Rivière et Cie., 1920.

—— "Pages inedites de Blanqui (1848-1852)," La Révolution de 1848, XXII (1925-26), 541-58.

—— Une Révolution manquée. Paris: Éditions de la Nouvelle Revue Critique, 1933.

—— Socialisme et communisme en France de 1871 à 1947. Paris: Éditions France-Empire, 1947.

Index